Prisone

SYDNEY EVANS

Edited by
Brian Horne and Andrew Linzey

The Lutterworth Press
Cambridge

In Memory of Giles Evans

The Lutterworth Press
P.O. Box 60
Cambridge
CB1 2NT

British Library Cataloguing in Publication Data
Evans, Sydney
Prisoners of hope.
  1. Christian life
  I. Title II. Horne, Brian III. Linzey, Andrew
  248.4

ISBN 0-7188-2819-4

First published in 1990 by The Lutterworth Press

Printed in Great Britain by
The Guernsey Press Co. Ltd., Guernsey, Channel Islands.

Preface

The sermons in this volume are arranged in chronological order, but were delivered in a number of different settings over a period of time spanning almost twenty years. These details are listed below for reference:

Contents

Acknowledgements

Our grateful thanks to Hugh Evans for his warm encouragement of this project and for copyright permission.

We are especially grateful to the Evans family, Mary Gold, and Gray's Inn for their generous assistance without which publication would have been impossible.

Our thanks to the Dean and Chapter of Salisbury Cathedral for allowing us to use their photograph of the Prisoners of Conscience Window, giving us access to the papers of the late Sydney Evans held in the Cathedral Library and for the assistance extended to us by their Librarian, Suzanne Eward.

Thanks are also due to the Centre for the Study of Theology in the University of Essex for their secretarial help in the preparation of the manuscript.

Brian Horne
Andrew Linzey

The publishers gratefully acknowledge the permission granted by Faber & Faber and Wm Collins Sons & Co Ltd to publish herein extracts from works by W.H. Auden, T.S. Eliot and Alan Paton.

Introduction

In the crypt of St Paul's Cathedral the tomb of Sir Christopher Wren is marked by a plain black marble slab. Inscribed in the wall above is the famous epitaph: *si monumentum requiris, circumspice*. Sydney Evans is not buried within the walls of the cathedral of which he was Dean, but it would not have been inappropriate to have had inscribed in the floor or the wall of the east end of Salisbury Cathedral a similar epitaph. It might have read: *si monumentum requiris, sursumspice*; for if one stands behind the high altar of the cathedral looking upwards and eastwards one will be looking at his monument: the five tall lancet windows filled with stained glass that was inspired and commissioned by Sydney Evans, shortly after he was appointed Dean, from the French artist Gabriel Loire. They are called, significantly, the Prisoners of Conscience windows; and they transformed the interior of that somewhat cold and sombre building. They have not, of course, been universally admired or considered beautiful - any more than another of his controversial acquisitions for the cathedral, the figure of the striding madonna by the contemporary British artist Elizabeth Frink, on the lawns to the north of the building. He loved the cathedral and the life and responsibilities of a Dean, and the sermon *Heaven upon Earth*, reprinted here, gives a brief glimpse into what he thought a Dean's role was and what he thought a cathedral should be. It also gives us more than that; it shows us how important the concept of Beauty was to him in his understanding both of the God he worshipped and the people he served.

The masterpieces of Loire and Frink came late in life. Earlier, when he was Dean of King's College, London and Warden of the Theological Hostel in Vincent Square, he had acquired two remarkable modern wooden sculptures on the theme of the sufferings of Job for the College chapel in the Strand. His admiration for the work of Barbara Hepworth lay behind the College's temporary acquisition of one of her larger pieces to stand (to the great astonishment of many) in the

7

forecourt. The sanctuary of the Hostel chapel was re-designed, at the request of Sydney Evans, by Louis Osman: the result was the controversial cross, known as the 'man-trap', the curiously shaped altar-table, and the candlesticks of a radically modern design in heavy beaten silver. His belief in the power and duty of the artist to evoke the splendour of God, to challenge a materialist society, and to enliven and refresh dull or weary hearts and minds was a persistent element in his life and thought and is a theme which runs, sometimes subliminally, through many of the sermons and addresses we have collected. He did not eschew theology, but when trying to illustrate a point of belief or behaviour it was to the poet or the novelist that he turned rather than the professional theologian.

However, it is not primarily by man-made monuments that he will be remembered; nor would he have wished to be so remembered. Indeed, when he came to speak of epitaphs he chose words very different from those which commemorate the architect of St Paul's Cathedral. Towards the end of the sermon he preached in 1973 in St Stephen's House, Oxford, he said: 'There is only one epitaph that is really appropriate on the tombstone of a priest: 'He made God real for others'! Bearing this in mind we can see that there is another sense in which the words commemorating Sir Christopher Wren are exactly appropriate to Sydney Evans - except that one should not be 'looking round' at a building, but at a multitude of human lives. Far more important than any of the artefacts for which he was responsible is the monument of the thousands of lives that were touched and changed by contact with him. It is hoped that this collection of sermons and addresses will give some indication of how he 'made God real' for others.

For the greater part of his life he was engaged in the task of theological education, and much of the material in this book reflects this work. As Warden of St Boniface's College in Warminster and later as Dean of King's College he was intimately involved in the training of men for the priesthood in the Church of England. On a broader front he was concerned daily with the life of the College and the University, constantly in contact with young men and women listening to their questions and sharing their anxieties. If some of the language of these sermons sounds dated it is because of his attempt to speak directly to the problems current in the decades between 1950 and 1980. He was, moreover, not simply an educationalist, teacher and administrator, he was a priest; and a priest who consistently saw his priesthood in terms of service both to individuals and to the community in which he was placed. His ministry stretched beyond the boundaries of student lives to those of his colleagues, to the lawyers of Gray's Inn, to the world of medicine, and to anyone who came to him seeking his help or advice. The sermons and addresses reflect also these wider concerns: the quality of the life of the nation as well as the spiritual condition of individual souls. The life of a priest is, inevitably, more public than the lives of most people in our society and more exposed to criticism. Sydney Evans was a very public man and was often criticised: he knew, as well as anyone, that the public appearance, if it is to be authentic, had to be built upon the foundation of a strong, inner spiritual life. The difficulty of integrating the two spheres, private and public, pressed upon him heavily and, sometimes, painfully; but public action had to arise out of private integrity, and private integrity, for a Christian, could only be the result of a combination of spiritual discipline and intellectual honesty. If, as Austin Farrer - a man Sydney Evans admired - once remarked, a priest is to be a kind of 'walking sacrament', one must be rooted in prayer and close to God. So, many of these sermons and addresses show him trying to find a contemporary spirituality; and one is aware that he often faces two ways. Like Paul Tillich, he frequently stood on the boundary: on the one hand were the questions being asked by contemporary society; on the other were the answers given by the Christian tradition. How could these be matched? How could one pray in a godless world?

One will search in vain to find a systematic theology in these sermons and addresses; each one was prompted by a specific occasion. Nor, it must be said, was he particularly systematic in his thinking; but there was a coherence in his understanding and practice of the Christian faith. He was criticised by those who wanted a harder-edged, more dogmatic kind of Christian statement and also by those who expected him to be more sceptical and liberal. He understood scepticism and doubt. But he was angered by those who allowed them to become an excuse for faithlessness and cynicism, and held fast to his own perception of the central tenets of the Christian faith; from his belief that in

Christ was to be found the ultimate revelation of God, and in the following of Christ the clue to authentic human existence. If one must attach a label to this kind of life and thinking, it is Christian Humanism: the conviction that becoming really human entailed the discovery of the meaning of the life, death and resurrection of Jesus Christ; and, conversely, that to be truly Christian was to become really human. This humanism is not to be confused with Optimism or Pelagianism. None of his sermons and addresses show that he believed that human society was inevitably progressing towards a better future, nor that human beings had the capacity to achieve their own salvation. He was, perhaps, more conscious than most preachers and teachers of the dark and terrible side of human existence. He speaks painfully of the frailty and brokenness of individual lives; and a recurring theme is the destruction and suppression of human beings by tyrannical political regimes: the arrogant assertion of the collective will over individual questioning - hence his determination that the glorious colours of the stained glass in the east windows of Salisbury Cathedral should depict the sufferings of prisoners of conscience. But at the centre of the windows, as at the centre of all these sermons and addresses, is the figure of hope: Jesus Christ, the one who suffers with all those who suffer; the one who, alone, is able to enter the darkest prisons of our lives to offer freedom.

Biographical Note

SYDNEY HALL EVANS CBE, MA, DD 1915-1988

His early education in Bristol was followed by five years at St Chad's College in the University of Durham where he took first-class degrees in both Classics and Theology. Shortly after his ordination in 1940 he joined the Royal Air Force as a chaplain and lecturer. In 1945 he began his long association with King's College in the University of London, first as Chaplain and Tutor, then as Warden of the Theological College at Warminster (1947-1956), and finally as Dean of the College in succession to an illustrious predecessor, Eric Abbott. There he remained for thirty years until his final appointment as Dean of Salisbury in 1977. He was Preacher of Gray's Inn from 1960 and in 1977 received the singular distinction of being made an Honorary Master of the Bench of Gray's Inn. From 1972 to 1974 he was Public Orator to the University of London. During his years in London much of his time was given to work for the Institute of Religion and Medicine, the British Association for Counselling and the Howard League for Penal Reform. In 1975 he was awarded the CBE for his services to theological education.

The Editors

Brian Horne is a Lecturer in Christian Doctrine and History at King's College, London and was Sub-Warden of King's College Theological Hostel between 1968 and 1978.

Andrew Linzey is Chaplain to the University of Essex and Director of Studies of the Centre for the Study of Theology in the University of Essex.

City of Men: City of God

I

To cross Waterloo Bridge from the south bank to the north on a late autumn afternoon when the sun is low in the western sky is to see the city clothed in a transparency of gold. Buildings are transfigured. 'Earth has not anything to show more fair'. And in that prospect I include King's College, London. We at King's can't complain if Wordsworth didn't have us specifically in mind when he composed the sonnet upon Westminster Bridge which begins with the line quoted above: His sonnet was published in 1807. King's was founded in 1829, but it was our building which completed the frontage of Somerset House which Wordsworth undoubtedly had in view. So whenever I cross Waterloo Bridge and my eye takes in this glory of buildings transfigured in the autumn sun, I think of Wordsworth on his bridge further up the river. But I find myself remembering also those older aspirations in which men have spoken hopefully of a heavenly city, picturing the city of their desires as a golden Jerusalem, a city whose builder and maker is God.

But on a grey day when your mood is low, the city seems to speak only of what is most depressing about human existence. To be on the top of a bus held up in the rush-hour of a wet winter evening by crowds of unidentifiable humans hurrying across the Strand to Charing Cross and the discomforts of travel to suburban homes, to be so placed is to be exposed to gloomy thoughts about this meaninglessness of life: 'so many people', 'to what purpose'?

All our human experiences and endeavours are shot through with contradictions and questions such as these. Always there's the contrast between what *is* and what *might be*. City life in London, as in every city, is what we know it to be; at one and the same time a fascinating and a depressing kaleidoscope of human life. The city soars to heights of cultural achievement in architecture, art and music. Athens, Rome, Vienna, Paris are names that stir our imagination as we recall what these cities have contributed to our western civilisation. Great cities are vibrant centres of creative activity where men interpret themselves to each other in theatre, church, art gallery, library, university, parliament. Every city is the scene of some new expression of human inventiveness and technical advance, a place where human relationships are protected by laws developed out of the accumulated wisdom and reflection of good men; every city is a place of commerce and government, where policies are formed and decisions made; a place where men and women fall in love and produce children and laugh together and become sick and die; every city is a place where neighbour helps neighbour; where you can find doctors, teachers, nurses, priests; a place where men in no small measure recognise and exercise their responsibility to their fellow men. All this and much besides makes a city the fascinating place it is. 'When a man is tired of London, he is tired of life,' wrote Samuel Johnson.

But a city also has its underworld; every city contains within its compass all the vices known to man, every kind of sharp practice, crime, cruelty; violence is always just below the surface. A city contains the sleazy joints of Soho, the crowded tenements of Harlem, the barricades of Belfast, the grinding poverty of Calcutta; the drug addicts and the meths drinkers, the lonely solitaries in bed-sitters, the mentally ill; and all those other people who can be said to be living but only 'partly living', bored most of the time, without expectation, without joy.

Nowhere are the deep contrasts and contradictions of human experience more sharply expressed than in the life of cities. But city life will be the way in which life will be lived by more and more human beings in the years ahead. The rapid expansion of cities is the inevitable result of rapid population increase in mechanised age. The urgent *human* question has become a question about *cities*. Can the pattern of city life be so designed that human beings can enjoy each other and become more genuinely human? Of all the practical problems for the future this is the most pressing. Time is not on our side.

14

Unparalleled threat hangs over unparalleled promise.

I recall that at another critical turning point in the history of our western world, when Imperial Rome was declining to its fall, there was a theologian in North Africa who wrote a penetrating diagnosis of those times and called his book the *City of God*. City of men: city of God. Augustine's conviction and hope sustained men through dark ages and helped them to create a new world. Does this idea of the City of God still have power to stimulate our imagination and arouse our determination and guide our action towards the creation of social patterns that will make possible a style of life that is good for human persons? Can we give George Canning's words a new meaning and call into existence the New World 'to redress the balance of the Old'?

As Christians we have a tendency to interpret Christianity almost exclusively in terms of persons and personal relationships. Nor would I want anything I say to be thought to diminish the importance of this Christian conviction about the primacy of the person. Of all Christianity's contributions towards making and keeping the human race more genuinely human, this has been the most influential. The Gospels, the teaching of Jesus, his attitude to others - all this exalts the individual in his uniqueness and high possibilities of personal growth. He makes us believe in ourselves because he makes us feel that we matter. In these days of ever vaster collectivities in industry, commerce, government when the individual feels that his voice and vote count for nothing, anything that can be done to rescue and enhance what is personal is urgent for human happiness and well-being. But if as Christians we focus attention and effort on the individual and overlook the influence of social structures we are in danger of abandoning the individual to his fate. Social structures, the organisations and institutions of city life, powerfully effect the lives of individual persons. Doesn't our full Christian obligation have a political aspect? Is it not part of our Christian understanding of responsibility to work for a public opinion which will demand of the government of the day a continuing reappraisal of national priorities in terms of human dignity and human need?

Every person is an individual with his unique identity and personal potential. But no person can live alone. Man needs a city. But if the city is distorted the individual and the family are at risk. Men and women and children can be broken in spirit by social circumstances too harsh for them to bear.

Awareness of the way in which social structures press on persons is growing. The social conscience of many young people today is ground for hope: they want to help the casualties of a ruthless world. But all this energy and effort of compassion is no substitute for the much sterner and emotionally less satisfying task of rethinking the very presuppositions on which our social order is built. Compassion is not enough. We have to ask what basic changes in the structures and priorities of city life are needed if as men we are to exercise a proper responsibility to our fellow men. It's not just a matter of feeding the hungry, but of educating and offering the opportunity of meaningful activity to all these new people who are being born in our world at the rate of 300,000 children every day. Without bread no man can live: but no man can live on bread alone and be a man.

If then we allow our minds to be open to those ancient Christian hopes of the City of God somehow transforming the city of men; if we allow our imagination to be stimulated by the vivid symbolism of the new Jerusalem; if we set out to rehabilitate these symbols and these expectations, shall we be accused of evading immediate responsibilities by allowing our minds to feed on fantasies? The idea of the heavenly Jerusalem will by some people be written off as sheer wishful thinking. May not the idea equally be seen as a *necessary vision of ideal possibilities*, a vision with power to stimulate hard thinking about the urgent social problems that face us? Can we ever take really seriously the idea of the City of God without finding ourselves socially and politically involved? We can't so much as think of the symbol of a heavenly Jerusalem as a true pattern for the city of men without remembering the broken and battered Jerusalem of history: Jerusalem became a heap of stones. It's when we compare social and political realities with ideal possibilities that we're made to see that even compassion for the casualties is not enough.

If there is no theology of city life, and by that I mean no thought about city life in the light of Christian insight, what kind of thinking will provide working models for town-planners? If there is no theology of city life what ideas will stir the imagination of city architects? Has anyone begun yet to ask what are the pre-conditions of the good life for men and women in the crowded cities of tomorrow? Is it not urgent that technology should be married to theology before it's too late? Time is not on our side: and never less so than today.

What then shall we do? Shall we wait like defeated men without hope for the horrors of George Orwell's *Nineteen Eighty Four* to overwhelm us? Or shall we explore eagerly and urgently ways of opening up the confusions and contradictions of the city of men to the strong regenerative powers of the City of God?

II

'God's image', 'City of God', 'Jerusalem' - what does this kind of language mean? Obviously it is the language of poetry; symbolic language not to be taken literally, but allowed to speak to our imagination, allowed to lift our hope above the humdrum and the mediocre to the vision of better things, a better way of life. The idea of the City of God is the idea of the ideal possibilities of human society, of the city whose 'builder and maker is God'. It is the idea of human community in which the claims of God are taken seriously and the presence of God is not ignored. The idea of the City of God is the idea of a society in which men and women - you and I - conscious of the presence of God, treat each other with respect, whatever the colour of our skin or the the size of our bank balance, because we are all held within the love of God: because we shall all die. The idea of the City of God is the idea of a way of life in which our personal, group and international relations are constantly exposed to the claims upon us of human rights, of justice, of honest speech and honest dealing, of disciplined freedom, of the obligation to help the human race to become genuinely human. Not money but men: not power but persons: and therefore money and power at the service of enterprises which will personalise human relationships. If men and women are to live humanly and not sub-humanly in our cities, then our cities need to be planned and administered for this purpose. This is what I mean by urging a marriage between technology and theology. With our present knowledge and skill there is no practical problem we can't solve, nationally and internationally. Enough food for an escalating world population is not beyond our powers: but it may be beyond our will, beyond our willingness to take the steps and pay the cost. Food is only one aspect of the human predicament. Compassion married to technology is not enough: but compassion will get things moving. What emotion other than compassion for suffering men and women and children has the power to release the necessary energies of mind and determination of heart, the power to overcome our terrible complacency?

There's growing recognition of the need for a marriage between technology and theology. Medical scientists are increasingly perplexed by the moral questions raised for surgeons and physicians by new knowledge, new skills, new drugs. Christian thinkers in their efforts to help men and women to understand themselves and cope with their lives in today's world are no less in need of assimilating the new knowledge and powers of science, than technologists are in need of assimilating those understandings of what makes life really good for men and women which are within the treasured inheritance and beliefs of Christianity. Science and theology need each other if men are to be saved.

Those of us who think about life as Christians have no blue-print to offer to social engineers faced with enormous problems of population increase, of spreading urban sprawls, of racial integration, of education, and of finance. Answers have to be found; decisions have to be made; action has to be taken. But can we doubt that it would make all the difference if those truths about human beings for which Christianity stands were to be in the forefront of the thinking of the men and women, at every level, whose attitudes affect policy and whose discussion precedes decision?

There are no final solutions. Humanity is always on the move: 'strangers and exiles on the earth ... seeking a homeland ... desiring a better country ... looking forward to the city which has foundations, whose builder and maker is God'.

There are no final solutions and there's no going back. We go forward, not knowing where we are going, into ever new human and social situations that call for intelligent diagnosis and courageous decision. Compassion for casualties on the journey is not enough: but there can never be enough compassion. The victims of man's inhumanity are always in need of more help than is ever forthcoming. Long-term thinking must never be allowed to take our eyes away from present suffering, nor must present suffering ever be allowed to take our attention away from long-term thinking. A Christian understanding of man's responsibility to man commits us to both. The presence among us of Jesus, born in an outhouse and executed on a tree, lays on us the double obligation of *generous action now* to relieve human suffering in all its many terrible forms, and *radical thinking now* towards a more human society. If we will do this, we shall become channels for the in-flow into the life of the city of men of the strong regenerative powers of the city of God.

Choose Life

I

The most important thing that has ever happened to us happened without our having any choice in the matter at all. A female ovum was impregnated by a male sperm and after nine months you and I were born. In the case of most of us this happening was intended: it was desired and chosen by that man and that woman who thereby became our parents: your birth and mine was desired, intended, chosen within a relationship of mutual love. As we grew up within this relationship we experienced - first unconsciously and then consciously - the fact that we were ourselves loved and cared for: and that experience has been an essential ingredient in our own inner security and ability to relate well to other people. But in the case of some of us this original happening was unintended: a few of you perhaps do not know the identity of one or both of your parents; you have had to come to terms with this fact; some of you will have been more deeply affected by this knowledge than others. Others of us were born of parents who desired and intended our birth but who, for one reason or another, have not been able in bringing us up to give us that experience of being loved and secure in a wise and sensitive relationship which is the environment of family life at its best. Such persons among you may at some time or other need help in coping with unresolved feelings of anger or guilt.

But whatever the circumstances of our birth and our upbringing, it all happened without our having any choice in the matter at all. And unless we are driven to it by some despair beyond our power to resist, we shall not have any choice in the matter of our death.

'You know what they say,' wrote André Malraux in his novel *La Condition Humaine*; ' "It takes nine months to create

a man, and only a single day to destroy him." We both of us
have known the truth of this as well as any one could ever
know it. ... But listen - it does not take nine months to make
a man, it takes fifty years - fifty years of sacrifice, of determination, of - so many things! And when that man has been
achieved, when there is no childishness left in him, nor any
adolescence, when he is truly, utterly a man - the only thing he
is good for is to die.'

This bitter remark was intended by the author of the novel
to be an expression of the futility of life. If human death has no
meaning, then the whole of life is nothing but emptiness. But
if death after fifty or more years of costly personal development raises this bitter question, what are we led to say when
we are confronted by the premature death of a young man like
Hugh Anderson or of a young woman like Anne Darquier?
Hugh Anderson, son of the Director of the Institute of Ad-
vanced Legal Studies in this University, died of cancer at the
age of twenty-one having revealed his quality as one of the
most outstanding presidents of the Cambridge Union since the
war, a young man of intelligence with a high sense of moral
and practical concern for the future direction of human society
and for the casualties of our present system. Anne Darquier
died at the age of forty having helped in depth a large number
of men and women - many of them students of this College -
by her skill as a psychiatrist and by her unquenchable capacity
for personal caring. Hugh Anderson had grown up within a
Christian family and found in himself a passionate concern for
the suffering of men and women less fortunate than himself.
Anne Darquier's upbringing was in total contrast: a rejection
by parents of whom she had good reason to be deeply ashamed.
And yet she so dealt with her own sufferings that what might
have made for hatred and revenge was transformed into
compassion and a rare capacity for understanding and helping
others in their varying experiences of rejection and alienation.

But what in fact has been the reaction to the death of these
two persons on the part of those most personally affected?
Not, as you might have expected, an outburst of bitterness in
the style of André Malraux at the mockery of death: quite the
contrary. The friends of Anne and Hugh have felt rather a

sense of gratitude for the privilege of having known persons of such quality. Their untimely death has fixed in our memories an awareness and acknowledgement of their worth which might have been only half-noticed had they gone on living. We have been strangely alerted from our contentment with what is mediocre and second-rate to a new sense of what it can mean to be a human person: our expectations have been raised, we've been given a kind of resurrection experience.

II

You and I didn't chose to be born: we didn't choose our parents or the environment of persons among whom our childhood was spent. We shan't choose the date or the manner of our dying. But in between our birth and our death we experience this mystery of being alive, of being human, of being oneself and not somebody else, of being this unique person.

What makes the difference between one person and another is partly genetic inheritance - what we receive biologically from our parents, partly emotional development - what we receive psychologically from our parents and siblings and others, and partly what we ourselves *do* with what we have *received.*

In one sense, you and I are not responsible for what we are: others have made us what we are. In another sense, unless we take responsibility for what we shall become - though being what we are - we shall never become real persons. This is only one of the paradoxical ironies of human life. Others are responsible for making me what I am, and yet I must take responsibility for what I do about this personality which others have shaped. To become a real person means taking responsibility for myself: the kind of person I shall be found to be at 30 or 40 or 50 or 80 or 90 will depend on the way I interpret what it means to take responsibility for what I am.

Our experience of other people teaches us that there is an infinite variety of attitudes that men and women adopt. There are the extremes of self-centredness and self-givingness, and all the gradations in between. There are wide and sometimes dangerous differences of attitude between one group of people and another group of people: Israeli and Arab; workers and employers; white-skinned races and black-skinned races; young people and older people. Even within the homogeneity of a group, political party or religious community, there is debate and disagreement. New advances in pure and applied science create new shifts of interest and energy in social life. Shifts in our criteria of relevance lead us to reject ideas and practices which meant much to our grandparents.

You and I find ourselves set to live out our life between our birth and our death in a period of unprecedentedly rapid social and cultural change. There's no *status quo* to which the more timid or the more conservative can go back. There's no going back. The ever-renewed biological energies of the human race issuing in our time in increasing control of the resources of our world sweep us on to the future. For better or for worse we have in our human hands as never before the power to build or to destroy. Sometimes it seems that we are set on a course to self-destruction either from guns or from garbage. Which will get us first - thermonuclear devastation or the pollution of the environment?

In this we face another of the paradoxical ironies of our human experience. We did not choose to be born: we shall not decide when to die. And yet, within the givenness of this life we did not choose, we find ourselves confronted by the need to choose between life and death - between policies and practices which make for life and policies and practices which make for death. Already these words 'life' and 'death' have passed beyond the merely biological reference: they speak of something cultural, moral, personal. There are many human beings today for whom existence is a kind of living death and very far from the fullness of joy.

Nor is this a new discovery of our generation trapped in the contradictions of a technical culture. We are simply discovering for ourselves in the context of a massive world population implosion and industrial exploitation of diminishing world resources what was seen to be the issue before the human race thousands of years ago when a Jewish prophet spoke these words:

'I offer you the choice of life or death, blessing or curse. Choose life and then you and your descendants will live: love the Lord your God, obey him and hold fast to him: this is life for you and length of days.'(Deut. 30: 20).

III

'Choose life.' This voice from among all the relativities and contradictions of our world - this voice addresses us in the very centre of our being and summons us to recognise what kind of being we are. Disregard this voice and we cannot achieve personhood. We are not just physical organisms energised by forces not in our control: 'naked apes' in the 'human zoo'. We are beings whose identity depends on taking responsibility for what we are and for the direction in which we move. 'Choose life' is a phrase addressed to us at the centre of our potentiality. A man's destiny is to *be* - to *be* as fully as possible what he is capable of being - and to *be* this at each stage of his development and of his dying.

But where shall we look for some interpretation of this voice? What is this *life* we are so deliberately to choose, this *blessing* rather than this *curse*? What does it mean to *love God*, to *obey him* and *hold fast to him*? Does this language any longer stand for anything real or relevant in a world in which we have become so accustomed to theories of ourselves presented in the language of biology and psychology?

There are several indications that man's understanding of himself in our time is moving away from the altogether too *simpliste* and distorting idea of recent years which reduces him to the level of a complex organism. Contemporary atheistic philosophies of man - both Existentialist and Marxist (Sartre and Gaeraudy are examples) - are using words like 'transcendence' and 'mystery'. Man is recognised as a being who reaches beyond himself, the depth of whose experience is inexhaustible. The gap between atheistic and Christian understandings of man is being narrowed. Marxist-Christian dialogue has begun.

I suggest that we shall find our way to an understanding of what it means to 'choose life' if we will allow ourselves to be really open to the future as it becomes the present, neither defending ourselves against it nor seeking to impose our own pattern upon it. By being open to life as it comes I include being open to what comes to us from the past. It is understandable if you feel impatient about the past in an age when engineers and technicians are so busy getting things done with an eye to the future. But we dare not cut ourselves off from our roots. We carry the past about with us as part of ourselves: this is true of us as individuals and true of us in our national and cultural groupings. It was a child psychologist who said: 'Tradition is the seedbed of creativity.'

The creative artist knows this. He draws on the tradition. He *infolds* the past in new forms of words and music. Benjamin Britten among musicians is for ever infolding in new and contemporary forms themes and myths and symbols from the past. His War Requiem, Curlew River, Prodigal Son take old themes and revive them in a new imagination. Among the poets we can cite T.S. Eliot and Edwin Muir. The creative artist draws from the resources of the past and so handles ancient themes that he thereby releases fresh energies into contemporary imagination.

What resources then are there from which you and I can draw to enable us to discover what it means to 'choose life' at a time in history when everything is in a ferment of change? How can we find and select and draw upon these resources making for genuine humanness and personalness in a world as confused and confusing as the world in which our span of years is set?

IV

The Christian is bound by the integrity of his experience to say in answer to this question: 'the basic and fundamental resource enabling us to be really human is God.' And that is a statement which either means nothing at all or else it means everything. To speak of God is to speak either of an illusion or of the essential dimension of the life we are already living - here, available, waiting to be recognised and acknowledged. God is not an extra to be superimposed upon all the rest that makes up our life. If God *is*, then he is the essential dimension in whom we live and move and have our being. He addresses us. This is the basic conviction of the Jewish-Christian faith. He is a voice speaking to us at the centre of our being from among all the relativities and contradictions of our world. He says to us:

'I offer you the choice of life or death, blessing or curse. Choose life.'

This is God's demand; that we shall take responsibility for what others have made us and for the direction in which we move, the priorities to which we aspire. He demands, that is, that we become men and not caricatures of animals. We must choose: and in this necessity to choose our *humanity* is made possible. Only by responding to this demand can we achieve personhood. For a man to become a man in the fullest sense he has to learn how to be responsive to 'the power not ourselves making for righteousness', to use Matthew Arnold's fine expression for the mystery of God. And if we do respond to this presence who addresses us with a word of demand, we shall find that the one who demands is also the one who enables. God who demands that we shall rise from our apathy and become men, is also the basic and fundamental resource enabling us to become really human.

To become human God demands that we come out from behind the barricades of our defensiveness: that we face life as it comes openly and undefended. Becoming really human is bound up with being set free from this need to defend myself, to justify myself, to create my own empire. Really human persons when we meet them are without defensiveness: they are vulnerable, ready to suffer whatever may be the consequences of being open to serve the truest well-being of others. This is the quality which attracts us when we meet it in a man or a woman who has it. This is the quality which attracts me when I pay attention to the Gospel-portrait of Jesus.

The practical quality of the life of Jesus is just this: he affirmed his identity by rejecting all defensiveness. This is the meaning of his suffering and death. Out of this dying of this undefended man there arose new resources of living for others. The effect of the death and resurrection of Jesus was

the making available for others of new and remarkable resources for living courageously and creatively. His friends
were transformed: they were enabled to emerge from behind
their defences and very often to die gladly for their faith: they
no longer needed to hang on for safety to old patterns but were
able to let themselves go into a new and undefined future.

What a tragic irony it is that in the eyes of so many of our
contemporaries Christianity is seen as a fuddy-duddy, out-
moded attachment to a style of life that is over and done with,
whereas in origin and in essence it is a dynamic energy making
for the kind of freedom and fearlessness which is most needed
in a time such as ours of rapid change and revolution.

Jesus stands in the midst of the human race as the one genuinely free person. He stands among us no less as one who
believed that human freedom is all bound up with recognising
that a man is a being who has to do with God. By the way he
related to God whom he called 'Father' he showed what kind
of presence, demand, resource, God is. He lived in complete
openness towards God in faith: he lived in complete openness
towards other people in love. He took life as it came, vulnerable without any defence except his own inviolable soul. So
severe was the challenge of this open, undefended person to
religious and political authorities barricaded behind their
orthodoxies and bureaucracies that they had to get rid of Jesus
in order to defend themselves. The undefended Jesus was
crucified by fearful men on the defensive. Jesus chose life. By
choosing life he was done to death: but his dying was the
moment for the liberation into the life-stream of humanity of
new and marvellous resources for living.

It is because I believe this to be true that I'm speaking to
you now. It is because I believe that there are in this Christian
faith and in this relationship to God in Jesus the Christ unique
resources for helping you to develop your own capacities for
personalness, in spite of all in our present way of life which
threatens to devalue and depersonalise and dehumanise; it is
because I believe this that I invite you to explore afresh or for
the first time the deeper meaning and possibilities of this way
of living which is called the new life in Christ Jesus.

But be warned before you explore too far. This Christian way of exploring and releasing life's possibilities is the most paradoxical and ironical of them all. On the Christian understanding, if we wish to choose life we have to learn to die in order to be able to live.

This is a hard saying: and many of those who heard Jesus speak turned back and no longer went about with him: they could not face life so undefended.

So Jesus asked the Twelve. 'Do you also want to leave me?' Simon Peter answered him, and a vast number of men and women of every nation across the continents and down the centuries, not least in this twentieth-century, have taken up Simon Peter's reply:

'Lord to whom shall we go? Your words are words of eternal life.' (John 6: 68).

Come and See

In his Christian oratorio entitled, *For the time Being*, the poet W.H. Auden makes the three wise men explain what had led them to Bethlehem:

> The first says:
> 'To discover how to be truthful now
> Is the reason I follow this star.'
> The second says:
> 'To discover how to be living now
> Is the reason I follow this star.'
> The third says:
> 'To discover how to be loving now
> Is the reason I follow this star.'
> Then they all say:
> 'To discover how to be human now
> Is the reason we follow this star.'

How many even of those of us who really are trying to live our human lives in a Christian way see it as an exploration? Somehow over the centuries timidity, fearfulness, defensiveness have changed Christianity from an exploration of life into a religion, into a kind of Judaism, into institutions which stifle the life of the spirit rather than release the spirit into life.

What has to be broken down before the power of the Christ-life can be liberated into the upsurging vitalities of new generations - what has to be broken down is the idea of the Church as an exclusive society. What has to be reconstructed is the idea of the Church as an open society to which all men have access. The 'Church' is not a religious club organised separately and in competition with a non-religious club called the 'World'.

What constitutes the Church is the recognition by certain human beings of what it really means to be alive and to be human in this world. The aim of Christians is to help other men and women to see what they see: to unfilm men's eyes so that they can see the real dimensions of the life which as men they are already living - living but 'only partly living' because they do not see what the possibilities really are.

Christianity is both a disclosure and a discovery of what is true for every human being. To be a Christian is to be a man - to be a woman - who has grasped the truth about the human situation and has been grasped by it. For the truth about the human situation is both a disclosure and a demand. Once you see this truth, this truth lays a claim upon you to adopt certain attitudes and to make certain responses to life as it comes.

Christianity, then, I am urging is a particular way of taking life as it comes: it is the way in which Jesus of Nazareth took life as it came to him and taught his friends to explore life as it came to them.

No argument can prove to me that this Christian attitude and understanding is the truth about being alive and about being human in this kind of world. As a way of life it involves, for example, putting other people's needs before my own. No argument can prove to me that I ought to put someone else's needs before my own. But Jesus the Christ, if I allow myself really to look at his life and listen to his words, confronts me with the issue so starkly that I am left in no doubt what it is that as a man I have to choose between. Face to face with Christ I am forced *to make a choice for or against love as the ruling principle of my life.* And what I would be choosing if I chose to base my life on love is defined for me by Christ and by those of my contemporaries who are authentically Christ's men and Christ's women. What is offered is no soft or easy option. The Christ-kind of living is personally costly - and yet a life marked by joy.

To respond to Christ as the focus and centre of my thinking about life and of my relationships with others means to be open to suffering, willingly vulnerable, but able to take life as it comes and do something positive with it. 'To be a Christian', wrote Dietrich Bonhoeffer from one of Hitler's prisons, 'to be a Christian does not mean to be religious in a particular way, but to be a man, not a type of man, but the man Christ creates in us.'

Today's preacher, attempting to read the signs of these present times, risks an interpretation of what he sees. He sees a deep, half-understood, inarticulate, often misinterpreted, yearning in the heart of many of his younger contemporaries for a better kind of living, a more genuine kind of loving, a more authentic truthfulness. He links what he sees with W.H. Auden's interpretation of it in the voices of the three wise men in his Christmas oratorio:
'To discover how to be human now
Is the reason we follow this star.'

Today's preacher finds support for his intuition that there is a deep stirring of human imagination and desire for a new style of life which will be more personal and more compassionate not only in what his younger contemporaries are saying and singing and doing - in social service for example - he finds support for his diagnosis also in what they are reading. How are we to explain the unparalleled popularity of Tolkein's saga *The Lord of the Rings* except as an indication that an ancient myth has regained its power? I mean that myth which represents the life of a man as a journey, a quest in which he must do battle with forces of destruction, in which he must take sides in the battle between light and darkness, between hell's angels and heaven's angels. If Carl Gustav Jung is right then these ancient universal sagas reflect externally profound internal symbolic movements and needs of the human psyche.

Tolkein's myth of the non-hero Frodo making his heroic journey with the ring that must be destroyed if humanity is to be free to live - this is but a modern casting of an ancient theme that life is a journey in which a man's integrity is forged and tested by fire. This myth occurs again and again in the world's literature and art and music. But for the Christian what is symbolised in the myth has become actual and real in a particular human life which is historically attested at the same time as it is theologically interpreted and made into the Christian way of telling the story which summons a man to awaken to his true nature, vocation and destiny. What recurs in human literature as a generalised myth has for the Christian been particularised, focused, epitomised and made actual in the life and death of the man of whom John the Baptist was speaking when he said to his listeners:

'There stands among you one whom you do not know.'
This unknown man is both Christ and myself. I know Christ - but I can never know Christ: he refuses to be captured within any theologian's analysis or any believer's imagination. I know myself - but I can never know myself: it is impossible to capture myself within my knowing mind. Christ is always surprising: I am always becoming something other than I was. But what am I becoming? What sort of a man? What shall I be like when I am old and others have to abide me?

What difference, then, does it make for a man to be a Christian? It makes this difference - that I deliberately and of free choice bring this unknown potentiality which is myself face to face with this unknown reality which is Christ. I expose myself in the depths of my being to this ineffable Other who makes himself known to me by way of disclosure and demand. And if I will do this with all my defences down and all my pretences abandoned, then there is the hope that I shall become what Bonhoeffer has called 'the man Christ creates in me'; and that man will be not a type of man, still less a stereotype, but my own self, my real potential self actualised into authentic fulfilment - a man, a woman who has discovered how to

'forget his selfish being
for the joy of beauty not his own.'

The next day John was standing with two of his disciples when Jesus passed by. John looked towards him and said: 'There is the man of whom I said that you do not know who he is.' The two disciples heard him say this and followed Jesus. When he turned and saw them following him he asked: 'What are you looking for?' They said, 'Teacher, where are you staying?' Jesus replied: 'Come and see'. (John 1: 35-9).

The invitation is an open invitation to us all.

Sound of Silence

I

In its basic meaning this word *silence* indicates absence of speech. Whatever metaphorical or poetical extensions of meaning this word silence may acquire in the world's literature, what the word indicates primarily is the condition when nothing is heard because nothing is spoken.

If then we adopt this paradoxical phrase 'the sound of silence' we are stretching language almost to breaking point in an effort to express what we experience when no words are spoken. When no words are spoken, the sound we hear is not the familiar sound of words, but the unfamiliar sound of no words - the sound of silence.

II

There is no silence more profound than the silence of a human person who has died. Nothing is heard because the power of speaking has gone. All we can hear is the sound of the silence of death. Whatever else All Souls' Day may have been thought to be about in the thousand or so years that it has figured in Christian calendars, All Souls' Day is about death and about the silences of death.

There is the silence of which I have just spoken - the actual physical silence of lips that once framed words and now frame words no more. There is the silence we feel in ourselves in the presence of death - our unwillingness to talk about death - the difficulty we find in writing to a friend who has been bereaved. There is the silence of whatever there may be of personal continuity beyond this physical transformation of which we speak when we say that he or she is dead.

'Where are you, my love? And in what condition? That

your body has returned to the dust, that I know. But what has happened to you, to your love and your warmth and your courage? Your dust is indestructible, but you, you yourself, were you also indestructible? Did you, you yourself, have no being apart from that body that has returned to the dust?'

'Where is your look of mischief now? For it was part of a miracle formed of dust, and now that the miracle has returned to dust has it gone for ever? Or is it, as it should be, a very part of heaven?'

So Alan Paton speaks into the silence into which his wife has gone - speaks, asks, but receives no answer - and yet does receive a wordless answer in the depths of his being, as you will find if you read his uniquely beautiful, painfully honest, genuinely human book with the title *Contakion for you, departed.*

III

I'm told that there are those who believe that they can accept the fact of death as they accept any other natural fact. Death is no more than the falling of a leaf. But I wonder just how many people over the years do in fact remain so detached. The death of someone we love has a way of disturbing us more than we might imagine until it has happened to us.

Sometimes an old person dies quietly in his sleep and we feel that is fitting. At other times death stirs in us feelings of anger. Sometimes, as at the end of a long and weary illness, death comes with an element of relief and thankfulness woven into the awfulness of separation, the sheer physical absence and emptiness. At other times the unexpectedness, the suddenness, the outrage hits you, stuns you, produces the physical symptoms of shock.

But always with the dying comes the great silence. What kind of sound is the sound of the silence of death? Is it a sound of emptiness? Or is this silence of death a *filled silence,* a silence more like that silence of which Pascal has written: 'In love, silence counts for more than speech.' Dare we so much as begin to hope that there is a word of love in that silence of death which so harshly separates lover from beloved?

I believe that most people find something profoundly perplexing and pathetic in the thought of a world process which permits and encourages the growth of moral personalities and then proceeds to annihilate them without exception. Mindless silence is a strange end of such a fascinating world.

The Bible, Old Testament and New, is ambiguous in its references to death and only obliquely helpful. Death is the enemy rather than the friend. But we are not allowed to dodge the fact that the one certain reality before us all is that we shall die. And at the very centre of the New Testament is a crucified man. We might almost say that the Christian interpretation of what it means to be alive and human in this world starts with a man tortured to death by the method of crucifixion. But if the Christian interpretation starts there it only starts there because of something which happened afterwards which made this death suddenly and supremely important. Whatever else New Testament writers are saying when they speak of the *risen Christ* they are certainly saying that out of this dying has come this new living. The transformation of their own attitudes, beliefs, hopes is sufficient evidence that there was something about the aftermath of the death of Jesus that was powerfully transforming and creative.

These men believed themselves, here and now, on this side of death, to be living with an energy of life that mysteriously came to them from the other side of death.

It is told of Francis of Assisi that when his doctor said to him that he was soon to die, he stretched out his hands and cried aloud with joy, 'Welcome, sister death.' In his last hours he added this verse to his *Canticle of the Sun*:

Praised be my Lord for our sister, the bodily death,
From which no living man can flee.
Woe to them who die in mortal sin,
Blessed are those who shall find themselves in
Thy most holy will.
For them the second death shall do no ill.

Francis could write of *the second death* because he had died a first death on the day when he came down from his horse to kiss the leper. It was on that day that he entered into eternal life. It was on that day that he found himself in God's will and it was in that will that he died. And shall we not therefore dare to say that being in that will he *still is*?

Death is as terrible for a Christian as for anyone who loves and who watches a loved one die. Alan Paton's book leaves us in no doubt of the terribleness of human grief. But for a Christian the sound of the silence which death brings - the silence when no word is heard because no word can now be spoken - for the Christian the sound of the silence of death is not a sound of emptiness but a filled silence which Christian imagination in art and poetry and music has made resonant with songs of angels and of the whole company of heaven who rest not day and night from:

'Holy, Holy, Holy, Lord God of hosts: heaven and earth are full of His glory: glory be to thee O Lord most High.'

What do we mean by this glory? We mean that where a bond is forged in this life between a human soul and his creator, where bonds of love unite a human soul to the sources of the life that is eternal, then that relationship is such that bodily death can't sever. He who is in that will this side of death is still in that will we believe beyond death. We believe in the communion of saints, the forgiveness of sins, the resurrection of the body and the life everlasting.

We do not speculate as to what this might mean. We can't penetrate the silence. The silence is inexorable. But to the listening ear of faith the sound of this silence is a voice which is familiar, a voice which says:

'Because I live: you shall live also.'

God and Goodness

I

How can I hope to speak helpfully to you about *God* and about *goodness* when I know so little about either? These words have to do with *being* and with *doing* rather than with *speaking*. But as words we do use them in speech: great words indeed, and powerful evocative symbols. Used by philosophers and moralists *God* and *goodness* can become abstract counters in an intellectual game. Undoubtedly there are moral and philosophical problems raised by the existence of such symbols and the long history of their use in our human conversation about the nature of things.

Charles Gore, once Bishop of Oxford, used to say that if only one could believe that God is good everything else would become easy. I've never been sure which is the more difficult - to believe in God as *real* or to believe in God as *good*. These two beliefs are not separate beliefs: but part of the difficulty in believing in God as real is the difficulty which the harsh experience of pain and suffering poses for a belief in God as good. Can God be God and can God be good and yet also allow all this suffering? Is this world the best God can do? And is it conceivable that an act of creation at such a cost in terms of human misery and wastage can ever ultimately be seen to have been justified?

Questions like these challenge the competence of the Creator as well as his moral integrity. Theologians write books in which they attempt to reconcile the antimonies and reduce the offence. Such studies sharpen the issues for our minds without resolving the dilemma. Nor are these recent questions. They have been asked ever since the human mind became aware of the incongruity between *lived* experience and *believed in* cosmic meaning and purpose.

Not to believe in cosmic meaning and purpose is no less difficult than it is to believe in cosmic meaning and purpose in the face of contradictory facts. It is at least as difficult to be an atheist as to be a theist. To believe in God brings you face to face with the element of chaos in creation: not to believe in God brings you face to face with the element of cosmos - of order - in creation.

I find this element of cosmos - of order - in creation far more impressive and widespread and coherent and consistent than I find the element of chaos. The earthquake, the tornado, the cancer and the muscular dystrophy offend us in the way they do because they are so out of character with the order and coherence of the basic structures of the natural world.

The sheer fact of our existence, of our self-consciousness, of the contrast between experience and imagination - all this raises in our minds huge questions to which our intellect can't supply the answer. No human intellect can comprehend the whole of which it is only a part. Always stretching out towards answers to the questions we ask, we have to come to terms with the unanswerability of many of these questions. That masterpiece of dramatic poetry, the book called *Job*, wrestles with these issues - and in the end, under the avalanche of irony that is the thirty-eighth chapter, Job has to allow that God is God and that it is sheer presumption for human minds to imagine that they can probe the ultimate mystery of meaning.

II

If you press this preacher to declare *where* he stands and *why* at this crossroads of *Either: Or,* I can only briefly answer that intellectually I find it less difficult to account scientifically for the demonic, destructive, disintegrative elements and energies in human experience than to account for the regenerative, restorative, reconciling elements and energies present in human history and counteracting the worst effects of evil. I can account for the forces of evil in human relationships more readily than I can account for the forces of good - *unless* the real dimensions of existence are as Christians believe them to be - a world open to the operations of grace and not self-enclosed as a mechanistic system. In actual fact things never wholly fall apart, the centre holds, anarchy is never fully unleashed. In the middle of a world war there are men working for peace. In the dark days of totalitarian Communism candles were kept alight to human freedom by men like Pasternak and Solzhenitsyn. A Hitler is defeated, a Stalin dies: the energies of life are never still. Economic need forces concessions from doctrinaire and nationalistic governments. And at the personal level we see men and women becoming lovely in and through terrible deprivation and pain. The mother who has rejected her daughter for marrying the man she did, can't resist the grandchildren and family relationships are restored. All around us are what Peter Berger has called 'signals of transcendence'.

Facing the ugly facts of evil and destructiveness in this 'world's well-weathered open' - symbolised at the centre of its life by the crucified Christ - the Christian community dares to affirm its faith in God and in goodness, dares to affirm that the forces that make for life and morality are stronger than the forces that make for death and degradation, dares to affirm that though things fall apart the centre still holds, because the centre of all the centres is that life-giving reality from which the universe draws its being. And in claiming this, the Christian speaks of the interior universe of the individual self no less than the exterior universe which includes the sun and all the stars. There are too many individual histories in which interior freedom has been achieved in and through suffering for any reflective person to think he has said all there is to say when pointing to evil and pain as final evidence against goodness and God.

III

When a Christian speaks of God he speaks not of some unimaginable reality outside the universe but of a recognisable reality mysteriously at work within the human situation: present within the process in the sort of way that a good parent doesn't just give birth to children but continues with them through years of growth and development - essential to that growth and yet enabling the child to become its own unique and freely motivated self.

But for an individual to achieve personhood, true self-hood, he must be free to choose whether he will co-operate with the creative, regenerative energies at work in the world, parent, shepherd, saviour, *or* give himself over to be an agent of the demonic, anarchistic forms of evil, the thieves and the robbers. I speak here of those who are free to choose, not forgetting those who have been so emotionally damaged that they are made unintentionally and inevitably into agents of destruction. To believe in God and in goodness then is to believe that creative and healing energies are at work in human life as part of the order of things.

Whatever may have been the use of these words *God* and *goodness* in the conversation of moralists and philosophers, in the conversation of those who dare to commit themselves to a stance of faith, *God* and *goodness* are *invitations* to *exploration* - exploration into God, exploration into goodness - exploration towards unlimited possibilities of discovery about the world, about other people, about oneself. Let these words evoke within you the prospect of unlimited possibilities of discovery and of moral and spiritual and inter-personal growth. So shall we move beyond morality, beyond philosophy into the realm of grace, faith and freedom - into expectations of change for the better in ourselves and in our society.

For when you are up against actual sufferings, morality and philosophy and the resolution of intellectual questions are of little help. To quote W.H. Auden's poem entitled *Whitsunday*:

> ... about
> Catastrophe, or how to behave in one
> I know nothing, except what everyone knows,
> If there when Grace dances, I should dance.

Christianity stands within the existing confusion of human experience as an *offered answer* to all who are perplexed by the 'baffle of being', not an intellectual answer to intellectual questions but an answer in the form of a disclosure and a demand.

Christianity claims to be a disclosure of the real dimensions of the life we are all already living, the dimensions both of the demonic and the divine. Christianity confronts us with a demand based on this disclosure, a demand that we shall take our stand within the divine and open ourselves to the movement of grace, allying ourselves with the recreative, restorative, redemptive energies of God - energies present and at work in the order of nature and of history, but focused and displayed in a human life in which the battle between the forces of light and the forces of darkness was fought to a finish in one man's obedience:

Christ is crucified
Christ is risen.

The issue is brought into sharpest focus in the crucifixion of Jesus. If *this* man can fall victim to the demonic forces what hope is there in this world? The hope lies, we say, in the evidence of the continuing presence and power of this crucified man in the community of his friends, as evidence of the sovereignty of goodness and of God.

So terrible are the forces making for destruction in our world that they will increasingly have their way unless enough men and women actively and at whatever cost take their stand with the forces of goodness and of God. To be a Christian means to have made a decision to identify with God in the age-long battle between the forces of light and the forces of darkness, between the energies which destroy and the energies which make for life, and to do this in the locality of his own inner self - of his family, neighbours and friends - in that locality wherever he is, at whatever time.

Wherever the Church is being true to itself it is the place where human beings confess and touch the deepest mystery of human life, the mystery of good and evil, and the grace of salvation available through Christ. Allow yourselves to believe this and you will have no cause to lack confidence just because the Church is going through a difficult time of necessary reappraisal and institutional change. Allow yourselves to believe this and you will suffer no loss of nerve but know instead the painful exhilaration of taking your stand at that point in the world's life where the real issues are being faced, the place where God is at work in history as creator, redeemer, sanctifier.

Allow these words, *God* and *goodness*, to be for you ever open invitations to explore, and so may you discover that the very pains and contradictions which cause some to deny God's goodness and others to deny God's being are in fact the route by which we come to know that God is both real and good.

Authentic Authority

I

Once upon a time the Bible was regarded as a sacred book with great authority. Once upon a time the Church was regarded as a sacred community with great authority. In those times an argument could simply be closed by the formula: 'But the Bible says . . . ' or 'But the Church teaches. . . .'

In times past these have often been matters of life and death: certainly for men like William Tyndale and Thomas More (certainly for men like Beckett and Laud who are represented in the east window of Gray's Inn chapel). A great deal of our British history has been shaped by various interpretations of these authorities. I often think that as Charles I tore across from St Margaret's Westminster to Oliver Cromwell standing outside Westminster Hall, Oliver might have been muttering 'The Bible says . . . ' and Charles replying 'The Church teaches. . . .'

You and I live in times when such 'authority' is no longer what people feel to be the characteristic of either Church or Bible. But these ancient authorities, Bible and Church, are not the only centres of authority which in these days are questioned or disregarded. The authority of Parliament, of the judiciary, of the police, of the teacher, of the parent - these authorities are no longer regarded with the same kind of deference and respect as used to be the case. And now even the more recently acknowledged authority of scientists and technologists has begun to be eroded.

We shall do well, those of us who are in positions of authority within these traditional centres of authority, to examine most carefully what is the nature of real authority.

II

The word 'authority' has as its parent the word 'author'. Basically authority means authorship. An author is a person who originates or gives existence to anything, an inventor, one who gives rise to something new. In common usage we have centred the word author on the writer of books, but the essential idea belongs as much to a sculptor or to a father of children. The word *authority* in its basic meaning speaks of the act of producing, originating, instigating.

Then over the years the attitude of others to what is originated reveals itself either as one of acceptance or rejection. If accepted, then there is given to the author or the authority a measure of respect as the originator of what has gained acceptance. There has to be credibility, confidence, acknowledgement.

So from its basic root in the idea of authorship the word authority carries the further meaning: title to be believed - title to be obeyed.

This is easily identified in the field of academic learning. If you decide you would like to know more about Chinese music you rummage around in an encyclopaedia to find who has written books about Chinese music. You get the names of one or two authors. You might then write to the King Edward Professor of Music at King's College and ask him if he would advise you on the most reliable authority for you to consult. And you would write to the Professor of Music in the confidence that he would not be holding that position unless a number of competent people had decided that he was a suitably informed, intelligent and reliable scholar to hold that position.

We are now able to make a further distinction in our search for a better understanding of authority. We can distinguish between *intrinsic* authority and *extrinsic* authority.

The extrinsic authority of the Professor of Music is the fact that competent people appointed him to the Chair. There is public recognition. But he was appointed because of his intrinsic authority. He has within himself, as a result of the way he had employed his time in many previous years, an intrinsic authority to speak and lecture and write about music.

Sometimes men are given extrinsic authority who lack intrinsic authority which matches their public position. We have all heard of the Peter Principle which argues that a man is promoted to the level where his incompetence is uncovered. Some generals in the event prove to be more effective than other generals in winning the confidence and loyalty of their troops. Some doctors prove in the event to be more effective than other doctors in winning the confidence and loyalty of their patients. Some schoolmasters, clergymen, parents, prove in the event to be more effective than others in winning the confidence and loyalty of those who are within the orbit of their authority.

Whenever men in authority exercise that authority in an authoritarian manner that usually indicates that they lack intrinsic authority. The more authoritarian the less authoritative. When the authority is afraid he either funks responsibility or pulls his rank. The weak man relies on extrinsic authority, the man whose essential authority is intrinsic sits lightly to external buttresses.

III

If in our times there is a diminishing respect for extrinsic authority this probably indicates a loss of credibility, a loss of confidence in extrinsic authorities who are found in experience to be lacking in intrinsic authority. Role and rank are empty unless filled with quality and work. It is in the public sector of life that the trouble seems to lie. What is being challenged is the adequacy, competence and credibility of persons who have come to be in positions of authority in central and local government, in tertiary and secondary education, in areas of industrial management and trade union executive. And the very availability of challenge and criticism by means of the mass media has resulted not only in a more exacting degree of personal accountability but also in exposure of personal inadequacy.

Less and less can authorities hide behind the trappings of extrinsic authority. More and more are they being required to prove their credibility and reliability in a public forum.

If our title to be believed - or our title to be obeyed - is to be respected, we have to win that respect: we can no longer rely on borrowed plumage from the costume cupboards of whatever stage it is on which we are set to act out our part.

I want to suggest that the right way to interpret the challenge of our times to authority as such is to see it as a challenge to those who are in authority to be better men - to be better authorities - so that the authority we have been given is authenticated by the inner quality of our character and professionalism. If we are to be able to examine authority in this sceptical, battered, bewildered, complicated, pluralist society, then we need to be able to see that all authority has to be self-authenticating. We have to win response and acceptance by our quality as men and as authors. Authority is authorship.

IV

If this is true of secular authorities, it is even more true of the Christian Church. If the Christian community is ever to regain authority - and by that I mean credibility, the right to be listened to, the power to hold men's attention to what it stands for and is saying - then it cannot rely on accumulated respect from the past or from its traditional structures and institutions: it has to recover authority by the self-quality and evidence of its own life.

Those who think that this can be achieved by the reunion of disunited denominations, or by the disestablishment of the established Church of England, or by any tricks or gimmicks such as bishops being televised taking exercise in running shorts in their large gardens, - such persons haven't even begun to measure the credibility gap which exists in the minds of people today between what the Churches seem to stand for and what it is like to be a human being, alive and bewildered in this kind of world and in this kind of society.

In St Mark's presentation of Jesus, the things he did and the things he said evoked a response of surprise and astonishment:

The people were astounded at his teaching, for unlike the doctors of the law, he taught with a note of authority.

(Mark 1:22).

But the doctors of the law were the accredited authorities of the time: it was the accredited authorities who were discredited by the contrast between what they were saying and the way they said it and what Jesus was saying and the way he said it. Accredited authorities will inevitably be discredited unless they can establish credibility in the eyes of new generations by their openness to change and their wisdom in responding to what is genuine in the movements for change. Static societies become stagnant societies. Every human institution carries within it the poisons of its own decay.

Jesus challenged the assumptions of the accredited authorities of his day, and the accredited authorities removed this threat to their own security by murdering the challenger. Why else was Jesus crucified?

That is why any Christian man or woman who is in any position of authority must always listen for whatever truth there may be in those who challenge that authority or the way that authority is exercised. The Christian in authority will know the dangers inherent in any position of power and will always be trying to take a detached observer's view of himself, listening to the voice of Christ which may be speaking somewhere among the voices of the critics. And of all authorities, those who hold positions of authority within the Christian community itself will need to be on their guard against a closed mind and a too easy belief that they must be right. Church authorities have so often been wrong. Christians have so often been prejudiced and blind, too often have our predecessors in the Christian community claimed certainty in matters where a more tentative attitude was required by the facts.

By allowing false ideas of the authority of the Bible and by allowing false ideas of the authority of Church authorities to be assumed uncritically we have helped to bring about a credibility gap, as wide as it is at present. Long, painful, patient re-exploration of our title deeds is required of the Christian Churches if we are to discover afresh the truth of which we are the undoubted guardians.

A century of Biblical criticism has produced on the one hand great uncertainty and on the other a rigid reaffirmation of authoritarian positions. But a Church in disarray because it is honestly seeking the truth is in fact a better witness to Christ than a Church in apparent order and strength based not on truth but on a fearful authoritarianism. In our present sufferings, perplexities and uncertainties, we are I believe better able to feel the sufferings, perplexities and uncertainties of all mankind - and out of this new search for the truth that is in Christ Jesus we shall, I believe, recover our proper authority - by which I mean credibility, the right to be listened to, the power to hold men's attention to what we stand for and to what we are trying to say.

I even venture to hope that a recovery by the Christian Church of its authentic authority will in time help others in the secular ordering of the world's life to gain a truer inner confidence and integrity - so that they may be better equipped in their various responsibilities to exercise authority acceptably for the encouragement of the good life.

The Political Prisoner

If you were the editor of a newspaper with pen poised on the 30th December 1999, preparing to write your last leading article of the twentieth century; and if you were of a mind to select for your comment the person who seemed most significantly to embody the spirit of the century now ending - the person who most profoundly symbolised and summed up the century - whom would you choose? Would you choose the astronaut, the entertainer, the scientist, the technologist, the tycoon, the athlete? Whom would you choose? I would choose the *political prisoner*.

'But why that person?' you will ask: 'Surely there has never been a century without its political prisoners: the twentieth century isn't unique in that.'

Precisely, and that is one of the points I want to make. The twentieth century isn't unique in any fundamental sense. Science and technology have changed much in our way of experiencing life and our style of living, but at depth humanity and human society is as it has always been. That is why in the twentieth century the political prisoner is profoundly significant and symbolic - because the political prisoner is the most significant person in every century.

The political prisoner is essentially the man or the woman who challenges the lie in whatever form, and suffers imprisonment and death rather than compromise the truth. 'Here I stand: I can no other.' But while in every century there have been such men and women, non-Christian as well as Christian, in no previous century have there been so many political prisoners as there have been in this century. Thousands of these men and women, valiant for truth, are unknown and unrecorded. They have spoken to the human conscience by the silent witness of suffering and death. But a few have been articulate, have put on paper what they have intended, what they have suffered. Such writers compel our attention by the integrity of words validated by suffering.

The letters written by the Lutheran pastor, Dietrich Bonhoeffer, in one of Hitler's prisons continue to reverberate throughout the reading world, piercing complacency and revealing humanity. Gonville ffrench-Beytagh's account of his arrest, imprisonment, trial and acquittal has now been published. His offence was that as Dean of Johannesburg, with the help of two Jewish barristers, he collected money to enable black African political prisoners to have legal aid; and to pay the train fare to Cape Town and back for the wives of black African political prisoners on Robber Island who were allowed one visit a year for one half-hour - speaking through a grille in the presence of prison warders.

Reflect if you will sometime on the influence of these two names I have mentioned. When establishment figures have been forgotten it is their prisoners who have been remembered, or they too have been remembered as the men who persecuted humanity's prophets. What would we have known - or cared - about Herod, Pilate or Caiaphas if it had not been for the lasting effect, on humanity's thinking, literature, morals and art, of Jesus whom they arrested because he was too threatening to their authority to be allowed to live.

It is these men and women, these prisoners for truth's sake, who are the most significant human beings of all time - significant in that they were made to suffer - significant in that they suffered in the way they did. These are the men and women who have upheld the dignity and improved the quality of genuine humanity. These are the men and women who have achieved real freedom.

Solzhenitsyn in his first novel, *The First Circle*, makes one of the prisoners, Bobynin, say to Abakamov, head of the security police and Beria's right-hand man:

'You made a mistake there Chief: you have taken everything away from me. A man from whom you have taken everything is no longer in your power. He is free all over again.'

Never before in literature has the political prisoner been given such a profound interpretation as in the novels of Alexander

Solzhenitsyn. What he celebrates is survival in the worst possible situation, and not just biological survival. He celebrates man's ability to survive as a moral being, stripped of all possessions and honour but purged and purified as a man. For this kind of prisoner, social and physical descent and degradation is the path to moral and spiritual ascent and exaltation. He echoes the words of an earlier political prisoner about another political prisoner who had preceded him:

He who descended is he who also ascended far above all heavens that he might fill all things. (Eph. 4: 10).

Is not all this the essential Christian understanding about the meaning of a man - the excruciating paradox that a man must die in order to live? True humanism is dying life.

This is what the political prisoners have been teaching the human race for centuries - a lesson so demanding of faith and hope that it is more than humanity for the most part can bear to hear. This is the very opposite of what we all want life to be like for us. The heroes of Solzhenitsyn's novels are men who, like the author, survive at great cost to themselves but at no cost to others. Beaten to the earth these men can still say:'We did not bow down to idols: we did not collaborate with our oppressors: we did not betray our fellow men.'

The inner thirst of Solzhenitsyn's writing, his overriding concern, is for truth, and for truth in the full Biblical range of meaning. Truth for him is not just factual accuracy - it means also trustworthiness, reliability, integrity. Such is the truth that makes men free. Such is the truth that authenticates itself. We can't afford not to listen to what such men say to us.

Three times Solzhenitsyn faced death: in war, in concentration camp, in cancer ward. Three times he survived - survived as a moral human being with sensitivity refined and insight sharpened. We can't afford not to read his lecture which he prepared to deliver in Sweden when he was honoured with the Nobel Prize. This lecture, which he was unable to deliver because he was afraid he would not be allowed to return to Russia if once he crossed the frontier, is now translated and published. It is called *One Word of Truth*. I venture to suggest that there is no more important piece of modern writing: it needs to be read and read again. This essentially Soviet man is also essentially a deeply religious man, believing and venerating the tradition of Christian belief as a repository of essential values in a bewildered world.

I end as I began by suggesting to you that if you want to find the answer to the question *what do men live by*? you can't do better than read the writings and contemplate the lives of the world's political prisoners.

The message of Solzhenitsyn and of those nameless thousands for whom he writes is all summed up in the words of that earlier political prisoner of the Christian history:

> We are treated as imposters and yet are true: as unknown and yet well known: as dying and behold we live: as punished and not killed: as sorrowful yet always rejoicing: as poor yet making many rich: as having nothing and yet possessing everything. (2 Corinthians 6: 8-11).

This takes us to the heart of Christian spirituality: and until you and I are taking this spirituality into our hearts, I doubt if we can be of much use to our fellow men.

Prisoners of Hope

The Christian affirmation about the God-dimension of the universe of human experience is essentially an affirmation about the future, an affirmation of hope. To be a Christian involves us in becoming men and women with our face turned towards the future. *In the beginning God... In the end God.* And therefore in every present choice we are to see ourselves responding to the leadings of God whom we believe to be active in history from beginning to end making the human race ever more genuinely human and inviting us to co-operate with him in the making of ourselves.

I would venture to say that being a Christian involves having your face turned towards the future! But when you think of the stuffy conservatism, resistance to change, closed minds and shrivelled imagination of some who call themselves Christians, some of you will want to call my bluff. Is it not an excess of irony to claim that Christians are by virtue of their faith 'prisoners of hope?' If 'most of society is in the caboose' of the runaway train of modern technocracy, 'in the caboose and looking backwards' - then surely some of you will want to say that if you're looking for Christians that's where you would expect to find them - 'in the caboose and looking backwards' - and if they have any thoughts at all about where they are going, these will be dream-fantasies about 'pie in the sky'.

The hope by which authentic Christians are captivated certainly is a hope which reaches beyond the narrow limits of the short human space-time experience. How could it be otherwise if God is all that Christians believe God to be - the alpha and the omega, the beginning and the end - and this word 'end' meaning not conclusion but fulfilment, the gathering up of all things human into glory?

Admittedly there have always been Christians who have 'multiplied litanies and neglected drains' and that is the basis of the Marxist gibe. But an honest reading of history reveals the Christian community all down the ages as a source of immense compassion and caring, pioneering works of education, healing, social reform. Prisoners of an ultimate hope, they have found in that hope a psychic leverage for doing what at various periods of history could be done to alleviate suffering, educate the mind and kindle the imagination.

What threatens us all at this present time is that by multiplying 'drains' and neglecting 'litanies' we have lost as a society that ultimate hope which is the only adequate source of an energy sufficient to give us the imagination and the will to tackle urgently and intelligently the very serious predicament in which we are.

Hope focused on God as believed-in purposeful presence and sustaining power drawing humanity towards its truest good - such a hope sustained the Hebrew people of Old Testament times through all the unexpected shifts of their national fortunes. In New Testament times this hope was sharpened in outline and given more precise meaning by all that new thinking which was sparked off by the life, teaching, death and continuing experience of Jesus present with them after death. 'Christ in you the hope of Glory'. They spoke of themselves as living already with the spiritual and moral power of a new age, they looked forward to the full flowering of this new age as a 'new heaven and a new earth'. Embedded in the texts of the New Testament is the ancient Aramaic prayer of the first Christians, *Marana tha: Our Lord: Come!* And the final book in the collection ends with the prayer: *Amen: Come, Lord Jesus!*

If ever a people was oriented towards the future, if ever a people had 'the future in their bones', it was these early Christians. They got their timing wrong: they and we have had to learn to live with this future hope in an ever-extended timescale. But hope they did.

'What we shall be,' wrote the author of one of the New Testament letters, 'has not yet been disclosed, but we know that when it is disclosed we shall be like him, because we shall see him as he is. Everyone who has this hope before him purifies himself, as Christ is pure.'(1 John 3:2-3). And what does it mean to purify oneself? It means - says this writer - to simplify one's life at the centre: it means to live with a single and undivided aim: it means self-forgetful concentration on the true well-being of others: it means loving one another with the Christ kind of loving - costly, crucifying but transforming. So to live and so to love is to be an agent of God in his age-long purpose of transforming the world towards the ever more perfect humanisation and divinisation of man.

This is our human vocation and our human meaning as Christianity understands it. This is the lead we are invited to follow whether we be scientists, technologists, social reformers, doctors, teachers, parents, priests. There is no enmity between the Christian hope and the thrust of technologists and scientists towards a better future. What threatens us all is the lack of communication between the two.

Christian hope points the direction towards which scientific knowledge and technological competence need to be guided if our fantastic powers are to result in our true well-being and dignity as human persons rather than in our diminishment and destruction.

What then is our task as Christians? The task of our Christianity is to celebrate man's true dignity and destiny, and to see to it that men and women are helped to become as truly and as fully human as they have it in them to become.

And what resources have we for such a task? We have the words and example of Christ and of his saints; we have our prayers - personal and eucharistic - by which we seek to touch the living movements of God's present creative work in our world.

If these seem to you to be ludicrously small resources with which to penetrate the imagination of our age and transform its sadness into hope, then I bid you recollect that the resources on which we draw are the resources of God, and that there is no way of measuring the potential influence of such a company of men and women as we would be if we could really open our minds and hearts to this vision and allow ourselves to become prisoners of this hope.

You and I are living at this fascinating and terrifying moment in history when human beings are able more or less to control the energies of the universe and use them for selected purposes. More or less, but not yet wholly: and in this 'not yet wholly' lies our peril and our promise. Can we control ourselves?

All around are indications that urban industrialism is a failing cultural experiment. In a variety of ways men and women are seeking an alternative society. Some of you in years ahead will be drawn by your concern for the future into the arena of direct political action; others of you will work for a reform of our patterns of education; yet others of you will as engineers or medical scientists or general practitioners or pastors give yourselves to improve living conditions and alleviate suffering during a period of change too rapid for some persons to assimilate without emotional and physical distress.

But if the death throes of our present urban-industrialised culture are to become the birth-pangs of a new society based on values, attitudes and structures more personal, just and humane, then all of us will need to be persons with inner spiritual resources sufficient to enable us to pass into life through a thousand deaths - such inner spiritual resources as Christianity opens up for us - 'as dying and behold we live.'

Our primary loyalty as Christians will be to no political programme or cultural revolution as such. Our primary loyalty will be to the Lord of the Ages who in Jesus the Christ has shown us how to live creatively in this world as strangers and pilgrims. We do indeed seek an alternative society; beyond the wasteland we seek the city whose builder and maker is God.

One question therefore remains: are we, you and I here and now seeking this city with an urgency of passionate yearning?

The Truth that is in Christ Jesus

i. For head

A

It is a characteristic of the story as a literary form that it speaks for itself. A story requires no commentary. The father and mother who understand their job read stories to their children from early years. Occasionally a child will ask a question. Mostly a child lets himself go with the story, imaginatively taking part in it, identifying with one or other of the personalities in the action. Of all art forms the story is certainly the most popular. More people can respond to a story well written and well read than can respond to a painting or a sculpture or the playing of music or dancing of ballet.

But not only for children are stories told. The great novels of our own and other nations speak to adult experience and adult imagination. By reading stories we are helped to live with ourselves, to live with other people. The novel helps us to understand more of life than we have as yet experienced: it helps us to come to terms with experiences which have come our way but have left us baffled.

And when the great story is turned into drama and conveyed to audiences by great actors, as is the case with many of the great story sequences of television, something very powerful and universal in appeal is released. In respect of material goods, this country of ours may indeed be heavily in debt to the rest of the world. But if we measure the mounting demand from all over the world for these story sequences, we can take some pride in knowing that the rest of the world culturally is in debt to us.

The story not only has a popular and universal appeal, it has also the power to leap cultural barriers - and to leap the barriers of cultural change over the centuries. Ancient classical stories of gods and heroes belonging to a culture wholly other than our present scientific, industrialised, urban society can still be read and enjoyed by boys and girls, and the Greek drama still speaks to us of the paradoxes and moral conflicts of human relationships. Philosophies age, creeds date, but stories remain ever fresh and alive.

B

At the heart of our Christianity is a story, a story which for all the cultural changes of twenty centuries remains ever fresh and alive. The story of Jesus vibrates at the heart of our Christianity. And it is that story which draws us together throughout this Holy Week. There are details in the story that puzzle us as when children ask questions about the details in a story which is being read to them. And we find ourselves asking of a Gospel, 'a story yes! but *what kind* of a story?' For we are aware as we read or listen to a reading of the Gospels that this story is not just straight narrative nor pure fantasy. As we listen we are made aware that it is a story being told always on two levels: There is fact - plain matter of fact, straight history, something happened; but there is also the setting of fact in a larger framework of interpretation. There is the story of Jesus, of Jesus in relation to other people, things Jesus said and did, things that were said and done to Jesus; and yet all the time you are made to feel that the story is a window into a world of meaning which has to do not just with Jesus but with ourselves. And it is this uncanny mixture of history and para-history, of fact and interpretation of fact, of past event some-how painfully and joyfully present and contemporary - it is this uncanny mixture in the Christian story which catches hold of our imagination and won't let us let it go, because if we've once opened ourselves to it we find we can't let it go.

On the face of it, it is absurd that the story of a man who lived at a particular date in recorded history should be found to offer clues to the questions which human beings have been asking since the dawn of human self-consciousness. These basic and persistent human questions can be reduced to three:

Who am I?

What may I hope?
What should I do?
Or to put it another way - What am I to make of the meaning
of my life when I know that the one certain thing about myself
is that I shall die?

Science and technology for all the brilliance of their
achievements have no help to offer me when I ask these basic
human questions. Nor can the human sciences of psychology
and sociology ease my puzzlement at the sheer baffle of being
- the strange and awful paradoxes of suffering and joy, sorrow
and delight, desire for life and inevitability of death.

But the story of Jesus - the story at the heart of our Christianity, the story that is rewritten and relived generation after
generation in the lives of men and women who open themselves to the insights and impulses of this story - this story of
Jesus does speak into the paradoxes and contradictions of our
human experience. It does speak into our puzzlement at the
baffle of being. It does offer us help with our basic insistent
questions:
Who am I?
What may I hope?
What should I do?

C

When we consider this story of Jesus which is at the heart of
our Christianity and is the pulsating heart-beat of our continuing life as the community of faith, when we consider this story
of Jesus which as we said operates always at two levels - the
level of history and the level of para-history - the level of
remembered fact and the level of transcendent meaning, when
we consider this story we realise that it is never a story about
Jesus alone but always a story about Jesus in relation with
others and the response of others to Jesus.

We do not know a Jesus apart by himself. We only know
Jesus as he was experienced by those who were his contemporaries. We do not have a Jesus observed by journalists, tape-
recorded by interviewers, every word taken down by swift
stenographers. The only Jesus we have is the experienced

Jesus - the Jesus who was experienced by those who came under his influence and turned towards him in love and not against him in hostility. We would have known nothing at all of Jesus if he had not been experienced in such a way that the men who came under his influence believed themselves gifted with insight and understanding which they must not keep to themselves but must share with others.

To the question, 'Why Jesus?', the answer of those first men and women of faith was quite simple and direct: 'He speaks to me with a word of life: come and see if he speaks to you as well'. They preached the Jesus they experienced. When they wrote Gospels they presented the Jesus they experienced. Their purpose was undisguised: the basic thrust of the Christian message is to generate action through a new vision. The writer of the Fourth Gospel is quite explicit: his purpose is undisguised:

> These things are written that you may believe that Jesus
> is the Christ, the Son of God, and that believing you may
> have life in his name. (John 20: 31).

Here then is history - *Jesus*. Jesus is an identifiable human person, a Jew who lived in the first century of our era. But such was the impact of Jesus on those of his contemporaries who were open to him and not closed against him, that their experience of Jesus took them beyond mere history. They resorted to symbols in order to express the mystery of this experienced encounter with Jesus. They called him *Christ*, they called him *Son of God*. The function of symbolic language is not to indicate some fact but to evoke an understanding, appreciation, and perhaps even to re-create a lived experience.

The Gospels are written to *express* and to *evoke* an experience, and it is as such that we must read them, open ourselves to them, allow them to speak to our imagination and our mind.

D

The truth that is in Christ Jesus is something different from the *truth about Jesus*. The truth that is in Christ Jesus is a continuing reality vibrant with life for us as it was for Peter and Paul, for Aquila and Priscilla, for Gregory of Nazianzus and Augustine of Hippo, for Benedict and Francis, for St Teresa and St John of the Cross, for Bishop Ken and Bishop King, for Pope John and Teilhard de Chardin and all those millions of nameless ordinary men and women whose horizons have been stretched, whose hearts have been enflamed and whose love has abounded as a result of this encounter.

The truth that is in Christ Jesus is something very different indeed from the truth about Jesus. If a man asks what is the truth about Jesus he is probably asking a question about historical reliability. Did he actually live, did he actually say and do the things reported of him in the Gospels, did he actually die like that, was he actually seen alive after death?

To questions like these there really isn't any answer to give except to say that all we know about Jesus we know from the response he evoked in those who found in the encounter not just intellectual interest but a deep interior perceptual shift and reorientation of attitude and aim, a new view of themselves and a new desire.

The primary truth about Jesus is the effect he had on those of his contemporaries who were open to his influence and not closed against him. And as we've seen they didn't put all this on record just as a matter of history and historical interest. What the Gospels offer us is not a human biography but an encounter with a source of personal energy which makes possible for us today just such an experience as was theirs who encountered Jesus in the early days of the community of faith.

Something laid hold on those men and women and transformed life for them. The evidence of the transformation is written in martyrdoms no less than in letters to churches and gospels. They went about preaching and telling the story in the confidence that what had happened for them could happen for others. And so it has been. This same something has continued to lay hold on men and women and has transformed them. And *why else have we gathered* here - and why else shall we be exposing ourselves this week to the story of the passion and death and resurrection of Jesus except that we believe that in so doing we too shall be opening ourselves to yet deeper interior transformation of attitude and perception: seeing the world with newly educated eyes; seeing ourselves - each other - with sharpened awareness of the way things really are?

E

Why else have we come except we desire that God in Christ Jesus will continue the good work he has already begun in us, setting us free from all selfishness and narrowness of mind and opening up within us our latent capacities for taking life as it comes and doing something creative with whatever comes and in whatever form? We come expectantly, believing that the truth that is in Christ Jesus can make all the difference to men's lives, and desiring that all the difference that can be made to our own lives shall not be prevented by any resistance on our part.

All four Gospel presentations of the truth that is in Christ Jesus operate on the two levels of which we have spoken - the level of event and the level of event experienced by others and interpreted by others. But it is in the Fourth Gospel, the Gospel according to John, that the level of interpretation is most developed. *Truth* is a key word in John's presentation of the things concerning Jesus:

1. Jesus in St John speaks of the Father as true - 'thy word is truth'. (3: 33).

2. He speaks of himself as true - 'I am the way and the truth and the life'. (14: 6).

3. He speaks of another counsellor whom the Father will send 'to be with you for ever even the Spirit of truth'.

(14: 17).

4. He speaks of this Spirit of truth as the one who will guide the Church into all the truth ... 'he will take what is mine and declare it to you'. (16: 14).

5. He characterises the evil one as 'having nothing to do with the truth, because there is no truth in him. When he lies he speaks according to his own nature for he is a liar and the father of lies'. (8: 44).

6. He identifies the evil doer by his fear of the light: 'for

every one who does evil hates the light and does not come to the light, lest his deeds should be exposed. But he who does what is true comes to the light that it may be clearly seen that his deeds have been wrought in God'. (3: 20).
7. He promises his disciples: 'If you continue in my word, you are truly my disciples, and you will know the truth and the truth will make you free'. (8: 31).

F

John presents the issue between Jesus and his enemies as an issue of *the truth* and *the lie*. Jesus in St John says: 'now you seek to kill me, a man who has told you the truth which I heard from God'. (8: 40).

Is not this a key issue always in human relationships - in personal and family life as well as in the open society and commercial and political dealings - which shall win? the truth or the lie?

In this Holy Week we desire to be possessed afresh by the truth that is in Christ Jesus. May I ask you to do one thing during this week - to take chapters 12-20 of St John's Gospel and read them quietly yourselves, some each day? (a) Read them as a child would read, letting himself go into the story with all his imagination alert and impressionable. (b) Read them also as the adult each of us is, never wholly at peace in himself or with others, never entirely simple and direct in his thinking or his doing, believing that there is more possibility of personal and spiritual growth than he has yet attained, longing deep in his heart for this better thing but hesitant, fearful, holding back.

Read these chapters with a prayer in your heart: 'Come, Holy Spirit of truth - come take the things of Jesus and show him to me afresh - come and create in me that truth which is in Christ Jesus'.

ii. For heart

A

What an intensity of feeling John conveys in this presentation of Jesus:

> Now is my soul troubled. And what shall I say? Father save me from this hour? No, for this purpose I have come to this hour. (12: 27).

The Fourth Gospel doesn't spell out the Gethsemane agony of Jesus in a garden sequence as do the synoptic writers. The Gethsemane issue and its profound emotional cost reaches us through such words as these:

> When Jesus had said this, he departed and hid himself from them. Though he had done so many signs before them yet they did not believe in him. (12: 37).

> And Jesus cried out and said: 'He who believes in me believes not in me but in him who sent me'. (12: 44).

The Jesus presented to us in the Fourth Gospel is no cold-blooded, unsexed, half-man. Feeling, anguish, exaltation - all are here. Put this Jesus of the Fourth Gospel on the stage of a theatre and you would need to seek a Shakespearean actor of wide emotional range and intensity to interpret what is conveyed in these expressive words.

How fascinating it is that in this Fourth Gospel which is the most profoundly reflective, theological, mystical presentation of Jesus, the emotional intensity of Jesus should be most pronounced. How else could Jesus have been found across the centuries to be speaking into the emotional whirlpools of our human hearts, if he did not know all men and had no need for anyone to tell him about man because he himself knew what was in man?

Greatly daring, we venture to explore the truth that is in Christ Jesus - for the heart.

Jesus in the head
Jesus in the heart
Jesus in the hands.

This threefold method of imaginative prayer was developed some two centuries ago at the Church of St Sulpice in Paris. We are adopting and adapting the sequence for our explorations in Holy Week.

Last night we were asking what the truth that is in Christ Jesus might mean for us - for the head - meaning imagination more than intellect. All our worst human failures are failures in imagination. Bernard Shaw expressed this in a famous question in his play about *St Joan*:

Must then a Christ perish in torment in every age to save those who have no imagination?

So we thought earlier of the power of the Christian story to speak, if we will allow it to speak, to our imagination - opening ourselves up and letting ourselves go into the story, letting it say to us what it will - without resistance. For the truth that is in Christ Jesus is no static philosophical principle of correct thinking or right conduct. This truth is an energy - a life-stimulating energy towards personal growth - claiming our attention, desiring to be known, seeking admission, offering nothing less than inner transformation, a new view of ourselves, a new view of the world. The basic thrust of the Christian message is to generate action through a new vision. Only by being made to see our world differently can we discover what is required of us to live more responsibly within it and towards it. For the characteristic thrust of the Christian message is to turn us outwards not inwards - outwards away from preoccupation with ourselves to loving concern for the true well-being of others.

But the new vision, the new way of viewing ourselves and our world, will not generate new action unless the heart is moved.

B

It was the prophet Jeremiah, centuries before Freud and Jung and their successors, who declared that the human heart is sick and deceitful. The immense service to our humanity of these early psychoanalysts and their successors is that they have discovered more about the dynamics of the human emotions and have opened up new ways of understanding and redirecting emotion. Emotional sickness must needs be cured if emotional health is to set men and women free to explore the truth that is in Christ Jesus and relate creatively with others.

I know it is all very un-British and un-Anglican so much as to speak in public about emotion, even worse to give expression to feeling. But the stiff-upper-lip philosophy does immense harm: people are made less real not more real, less honest not more honest. They are prevented from being real to each other and the amount of sheer unhappiness and wretchedness experienced as a result of this false attitude towards emotion is incalculable. Emotional illness in adult life can be caused by the suppression of anger that would be better given outlet. More severe illness can result from that strange mechanism of emotional repression that occurs in infancy when children for whatever reason are deprived of the security of deep, unconditional, reassuring love and are afraid to let their anger out.

We are not told in the New Testament that we must not be angry. Indeed, it is John in the Fourth Gospel who presents us with the angry Jesus clearing out the money changers from the Temple:

And making a whip of cords, he drove them all out of the temple: and he told those who sold pigeons, 'Take these things away; you shall not make my Father's house a house of trade'. His disciples remembered that it was written: 'Zeal for thy house will consume me.' (2: 15-18).

The anger of Jesus was at all that he found false in the religion of his day.

Nor does Paul tell us not to be angry. What he tells us is, 'Be angry - but sin not'. And that's very difficult. Righteous anger - true anger against falsehood, against injustice, against drug pushers and land speculators, and all who exploit their fellow man - righteous anger is not easy to sustain without it going wrong. And yet a Church more angry with the anger of Christ at those things in our society which spoil life for others would be a Church more worthy of respect, more deserving of men's attention.

Of course there is anger within the Christian community - a lot of anger - but it is more often sick anger than righteous anger. It is not anger directed towards those who do damage to other people. It is self-centred anger, anger at having to face change, anger at having to change one's habits of thought or behaviour, anger at the suggestion that this Church-building must be demolished or these parishes united into a new group of parishes, or at this person given more attention than me. This kind of anger, this sick anger, has nothing to do with the conflict between truth and falsehood. It has to do with the fearfulness of the closed mind which cannot be open to new facts and new needs in a changing world. This anger is the anger of fear not the anger of faith.

When in any gathering of people a person reveals a disproportionate amount of angry feeling in connection with a particular cherished position of doctrine or practice, then what we observe is usually a reaction of fear: an indication of unresolved interior conflict.

The unhealthiness of some of our Church life - the lack of positive growth in all our lives - can often be traced to the presence of *bad feeling* which has not yet been changed into *true feeling*. But if we will really allow the truth that is in Christ Jesus to penetrate our hearts then what will be generated in our hearts will be true feeling - and in a new openness we shall be able to speak what we feel.

The weight of this sad time we must obey,
Speak what we feel, not what we ought to say.

C

Let me relate to you a description of what it means to be the Church-community of faith written by that deeply perceptive and learned Christian man, Clement Hoskyns:

The true function of the Church is to bring men and women into the presence of God and to believe confidently that a new love and a new charity will thereby be formed in them. Only when our religion can foster such ultimate morality have we a right to hope that England will be a better country or that we shall be better citizens, or that employers and employed will work together for the common good, or that parents will adequately provide for the education of their children.

Of course there is a new love and a new charity at work within our Christian community; there is true feeling reaching out into the life of our nation in the persons of committed Christians whose caring is a blessing to all within its radiance. True love is indeed gloriously in circulation among us: but not all that is in circulation among us is yet true love.

We can but start with ourselves: we can this week bring our feelings and allow them to be confronted with the truth that is in Christ Jesus. We can this week ask the Spirit of truth to search out all the bad feeling and the sick emotion in our hearts which prevents us from being open and real and unafraid. All that bitterness; all that resentment; all that unacknowledged anger - bring it out from the darkness of concealment into the light of confession - tell it out to the Holy Spirit and ask him to wash out our hearts with the pure waters of his love so that there may be no more bad feeling in us, but only new space and new desire for good feeling, for true feeling.

D

Call to mind those quaint but wonderfully illuminating words of the mediæval author of the *Cloud of Unknowing*:

Swink and sweat in all that thou canst and mayest for to get thee a true knowing and feeling of thyself as thou art. And then, I trow, soon after that, thou wilt get thee a true knowing and feeling of God as he is.

A *true* knowing and a *true* feeling. How this word *true* and this word *truth* persist in our search this week into the meaning of our lives and the direction of this development. Christianity, as I understand it, is all about growth, about development, about becoming what we are not yet but which we are capable of becoming. The truth that is in Christ Jesus challenges us to become more committed to growth in a particular direction outward toward others; and to express this growth in more responsible action. 'Self becoming' therefore 'for self giving'. Or as Jesus in St John expresses it in the prayer in Chapter 17: 'For their sake I consecrate myself: that they also may be consecrated in truth'. (17: 19).

'The only value my life can have is the value that others find in it'. So wrote Dag Hammarskjöld in his intimate diary, *Markings*. But how can my life have value for others unless it has value in itself? What is this value? What it is that others value in ourselves we can never really know. What we can know is what we find valuable in others. We can reflect on this. Look back over your life and ask who are the people who have contributed most to your own true growth as a person - who has helped you most profoundly at the level of deep inner emotional attitudes and needs at a time of crisis, decision, illness, bereavement: who has given you a new vision of your possibilities as a person - a new courage to go on and cope with problems and not to give up or dodge the issue? What was it about these people which enabled them to get so near in understanding your real need that they were able to speak into your real need and help you to see it with new eyes and face it with new hope?

Will you not find as you reflect on these persons in your life that they not only cared about you as a person, loved you enough to want to help you discover your true self and your true possibilities, accepted you even though you felt yourself unacceptable - will you not find that what you valued in these agents of grace was not only this special kind of loving but *within this love* a *special kind of knowing*, a feeling kind of knowing, a knowing from the heart, sensitive, unsentimental, honest, direct, true - yet gentle. Sometimes you experienced in what they said to you the sharpness of a surgeon's knife but always also the gentleness of a surgeon's hand.

They helped you to a true knowing and a true feeling of yourself as you were and yet always in relation to what they saw you capable of becoming.

How different all this is from the cruel, malicious, mocking criticism of other people, snide and cynical, that makes up so much of human relationships in our world! The only help that really helps is *truth spoken in love*, truth spoken from a heart of pure feeling of concern for another's well-being. Truth hurts: nothing is harder for us than to face reality, the way things are really all masks off, all defences down, no room any more for pretence. But if we can hear truth spoken in love and assimilate it into our own hearts then we shall come to know what it means when Jesus says in St John: 'You will know the truth and the truth will make you free'. (18: 31).

Free from all acting a part, free from all fear, free from all pretence, free from all defensiveness - and therefore free for open and unafraid relationships with other people, free for all your potential of growth into a Christ kind of loving, free to become a person whose life will have value for others. Such is the power of the truth in Christ Jesus if we will allow that truth to penetrate into our heart.

iii. For hand

A

Our theme is the truth that is in Christ Jesus: the truth that is in Christ Jesus *for us*; the truth which is to become actual in our very *being* - a regulating impulse and energy in head and heart and hands; truth in him which is to become truth in us - an intrinsic energy of truth to lead us out of confusion about the meaning of our lives towards insight into the true meaning of our lives. *Jesus in the head; Jesus in the heart; Jesus in the hands.* And yet no substitution: no obliteration of *my* self by another self but rather the very process by which I become *my true self* - the self I am capable of becoming through the transformation of my inner attitudes and feelings - the renewing of the spirit of our minds; the putting on of a new nature created after the likeness of God in true righteousness and holiness.

All this marvellous prospect is opened out for us in John's presentation of Jesus - a new view of ourselves in the vision of God which is made present to us in Jesus. 'He who has seen me has seen the Father'. And of the Father Jesus in St John says:

As the Father has life in himself so he has granted the Son also to have life in himself. (5: 26).

and again in another place he says:

I do not say to you that I shall pray the Father for you: for the Father himself loves you, because you have loved me and have believed that I come from the Father.

(16: 26-28).

And so:

Jesus knowing that the Father had given all things into his hands and that he came from God and was going to God, rose from supper, laid aside his garments and girded himself with a towel; then he poured water into a basin and began to wash the disciples feet. (13: 3-5).

71

John presents the truth that is in Christ Jesus as a point of intersection between the timeless and time. Here is *reality that abides* in the midst of all else that comes into existence for a brief span and then passes away. Here is a flow of real life from the Father who has being in himself into Jesus and through the human historical obedience of Jesus in life and death out into the lives of his friends by the inflowing into them of the Spirit of truth who is the Lord and Giver of life to us. So that we - the continuing community of the Holy Spirit across the centuries - are open to the inflow of this truth and this life here and now; and our understanding of the truth that is in Christ Jesus is expanded so that we, the Church today, find ourselves jointly engaged with Christ in the power of the Spirit, set in the midstream of the world's life to bring knowledge of this saving truth to mankind.

This is no private salvation offered to us for our private satisfaction. If we respond to what is offered, we are caught up in the cosmic purposes of God for the world's salvation. There is *work* to be done. There are *feet* to be washed. The truth that is in Christ Jesus for our *hands* includes a basin and water and a towel.

There is work to be done: we have to *do* the truth.

Nothing makes it clearer that what the Fourth Gospel means by this recurring word *truth* is something far other than an abstract principle of reason. Nothing makes it clearer than the affirmation that the truth is a way of life, *something to be done*.

To repeat what I have said before, the basic thrust of the Christian message - the Word of God which Jesus is - the basic thrust is to *generate action through a new vision* - a new being issuing in a new doing, a new way of *being* in the life of the world, Christ's *way* of *being* reproduced in our becoming as he is in the here and now of our circumstances.

1. In the cross currents of forces which in the world of our time make for light or for darkness Jesus says:

I am the light.

2. In the cross currents of forces which in the world of our time make for life or for death Jesus says:

I am the life.

3. In the cross currents of the forces which in the world of our times make for truth or for falsehood Jesus says:
I am the truth.

B

What then is this work which he puts into our hands to do, if it is not to *stand* in the cross currents of the contradictions of the world of our time *where he stands* - 'he in us and we in him' standing for light, for life, for truth - and sustained. Yes, but how sustained? How enabled to stand and not be drowned in the cross currents and the contradictions of our personal circumstances no less than of our political confusions? How else to stand except by the power of love, his life in us as we allow our frail love to be fortified by the daily receiving in us of his strong love?

C

The work that is given to the Christian to do is to attend to whatever human need presents itself within the reach of our hands. The mass media bring the immense problems of the world's sufferings into our homes. We are bombarded by claims on our compassion that we can't cope with. And the danger of this mass bombardment of our individual compassion by the intolerable burdens of humanity and the unending tasks needing the attention of world organisations and national governments is that we fail to notice human suffering and need much nearer to hand - and certainly within our power to do something about. We shall keep the antennae of our sensitivity alert for signals of human need in areas close to us. Sometimes what is needed is that willingness to listen and that capacity to love, to understand with a knowing from the heart. It is a Christian work to be a centre of caring and genuine human understanding in the neighbourhood of our ordinary days. Examine yourself in the matter of your exercise of Christian neighbourliness.

You will have found as I continually find a lovely readiness and desire on the part of many of our younger contemporaries to be of help to people in need. I believe that as a Church we should be encouraging more of the young to train for the several caring professions - doctors, nurses, social workers, school teachers: and I do not see how the truth that is in Christ Jesus can be continuingly presented to new generations of men and women unless enough and good enough men and women are trained for full-time ministries within the life of the Christian community itself.

Jesus in the hands - yes! all this that I have been indicating - the work of healing and the work of educating is the forever unfinished task.

D

But beyond the immediate individual and personal needs, beyond the national provision of hospitals and medical services and schools and universities, beyond the staffing needs of these essential institutions of caring and civilisation there must be a concern - a Christian concern - for *civilisation itself*. That things are changing is so obvious that it calls for no elaboration. New wine requires new bottles. But the provision of new bottles - new national and international agencies and institutions capable of enabling the surging millions to live and to live humanly - this task is daunting even to the bravest hearts.

I want only to suggest - and I can do no more than suggest for the working out of such a programme requires a meeting of many minds - that an international Christian initiative, possible now in these ecumenical days, might somehow be started for the purpose of awakening us all to the great dangers we are in from divisions even more unhappy than our previous and still-persisting Christian divisions. The divide of which I speak is a divide at the very base of civilisation itself - the divide between *science, subjectivity* and *sanctity*.

Science, subjectivity and sanctity are three universal human languages.

1. *Science*, the methods of science, the application of science, is a universal human language which in the past century has transformed and continues to transform human life on this

planet. Molecular biology is a science, a knowledge so basic that it is the same in South America as it is in Japan. Scientists meet in international conferences and understand each other. And there are growing signs - and not a moment too soon - that scientists are accepting something of their immense moral responsibility for guiding the nations in the right use of these vast powers. But there is a long way to go. National political interests are usually more persuasive than international scientific professional interests. The risk that we shall destroy ourselves is the risk with which we live. But the risk will be diminished if the language of science can be brought into closer contact with the language of subjectivity.

2. The language of *subjectivity*, the speech of the human imagination and the human heart, expresses itself in painting and sculpture, in music, in literature. Literature and art are international languages no less than the language of science. Printing, travel, television make separated peoples and cultures aware of each other's subjectivity.

The language of subjectivity rises out of those human questions which I've explored earlier:

Who am I?

What may I hope?

What should I do?

And high among the poetry and the prose of human literature are the writings of the world religions, including the writings of the Hebrew and the Christian scriptures.

3. But third among the international languages of men is what I have called the language of *sanctity*, which in a wide diversity of forms - goodness, holiness, saintliness, has found expression within the cultures and religions of humanity. These expressions of goodness, holiness, saintliness speak to something in most men and women - his and her own vision of a better self.

Buddha, Muhammad, Jesus.

Gandhi, Albert Schweitzer, Martin Luther King.

Benedict, Francis, Teresa.

I have only to mention such names as these to make clear what I mean by the international language of sanctity.

E

Here are the ingredients of human civilisation now and in the future:

the objectivity of science,

the subjectivity of literature,

the vision of holiness.

Shall we not see an essential correspondence between the three languages of human civilisation - science, subjectivity and sanctity - a correspondence between these three and the Christian symbol of ultimate reality as Father, Son and Holy Spirit - Creator, Redeemer, Sanctifier?

The human language of science is the exploration of the province of the Creator.

The human language of subjectivity is the exploration of the province of the Redeemer.

The human language of sanctity is the exploration of the province of the Sanctifier.

But whereas in the Christian understanding of what is Real, these three are One - three differentiations of essential Unity, Three Persons in One God - in our contemporary human experience and predicament there is a fatal brokenness, separation, division. These three international languages are not understood as three elements in a single human search for meaning, nor as three ways in which essential unity finds expression.

That rugged and eminent Victorian, T.H. Huxley, was no advocate of two cultures. 'Science and Literature,' he said, 'are not two things but two aspects of the same thing'. And his grandson Aldous spent much of his life as an agnostic in search of his God, prevented - as he said towards the end of his life - by 'the rationalistic formation of my mind'.

In our world today science is divorced from literature: neither science nor literature have much interest in sanctity. Our danger is very great. If scientists and artists are unable to acknowledge each other's right to live and mutual need of each other, our human nature will be split in an irreconcilable opposition. Truth in our Christian understanding is not *either/or* but *both/and* - not irreconcilable opposition, but creative tension - reciprocity, complementariness. Diversity in unity: unity in diversity is our Christian belief about the way things are.

But a marriage of science and literature in a reciprocal tension is still not enough. The basic human questions - man's age-long search for meaning - Who am I? What may I hope? What should I do? - these questions clamour for answer - and the only answer that can meet the need is the invitation to pilgrimage: 'You are a being who above all else has to do with God: a being loved by God and invited by God to share with him in the making of yourself.'

In response to this vision and to this invitation human objective scientific learning and human interior search for meaning are given a direction and a goal - a goal worthy of man's total allegiance and commitment. This bringing together into a new integration of science, subjectivity and sanctity is, I am suggesting, the great work which is being given to the Christian Church to do for humanity. Who else has the vision or the resources for doing it?

This unifying of human life must begin with what parents tell children in the home: it must continue with teachers in the schools and clergy in the parishes: others must take up the theme in books and in the media.

F

This unitive vision in which nature, human nature and the spiritual human nature are displayed in their diversity and their coherence will be acted out in the Cathedral when we celebrate the Eucharist of Maundy Thursday.

We shall bring bread and wine, material symbolising the area of scientific exploration.

We shall remember the events that issued in the crucifixion of Jesus, material symbolising the area of subjective human experience.

We shall stretch out empty open hands to receive the Bread of Heaven in Christ Jesus and the Blood of Jesus in the Cup of Life, the food and drink of our sanctification.

And on our lips and in our heart the prayer:
Come, Lord Jesus
Be in me
All that Thou
Wouldst have me be.

Invitation to a Dance

I

Among the paintings in the Wallace Collection in Hertford House, Manchester Square in this city of London - a city rich beyond measure in artefacts of human artistry and inventiveness - is a work by the seventeenth-century French artist Nicholas Poussin called *A Dance to the Music of Time*. Four dancing girls represent the four seasons of the year, while old Father Time calls the tune on his lyre. The girls dance hand in hand forming a ring, but facing outwards. The figure of Time the musician crouches over his instrument, a sinister rather than a kindly figure: Time that mocks man rather than Time man's friend. The painting is symbolic after one of the styles of those times, an allegory, intended to alert the imagination of the viewer and lead him to reflect on the human condition.

The reflection evoked by this painting in one viewer shaped his future course. This was the painting that set Anthony Powell going on his long writing journey of twenty-five years in the production of a sequence of twelve novels with the general thematic title *A Dance to the Music of Time*. Started in 1949, the sequence ends with the publication of the last novel entitled *Hearing Secret Harmonies*. A critic has called the novels: 'a joyful song about the endless curiosity and comedy of the world.'

Curiosity and comedy: these two words encompass a wealth of human experience. If curiosity is the driving force behind scientific research with all its applied consequences of good and ill, comedy is the content of literature, art, history. Comedy? Do I really mean comedy? Comedy rather than tragedy? Yes! I want to say that the tragedies of human experience occur within the movement of the comedy rather than to say that comedy provides occasional moments of light relief in an otherwise tragic theme. William Shakespeare saw

79

this right and clear. The comic scenes in his tragedies are not occasional moments of light relief: they are in his vision reminders to the audience of the continuing flow of normal human relationships. Life flows on: the tragic events arise out of and happen within the continuing usual comedy. The medieval imagination, of which Shakespeare is heir saw life so, as many a mystery play and illuminated missal declares. Which is hardly surprising: for this is itself a reflection of the Christian imagination composed over the centuries from the recurring counterpoint of Christ crucified and Christ risen. Christians interpret life not as human tragedy but as divine comedy: divine comedy at the heart of which is a crucified man. Suffering and death in the Christian interpretation do not have the last word. Fullness of life is entered only by way of a thousand deaths to half-life curved in on itself. Gospel life properly perceived is the offer of salvation from that half-life curved in on itself which T.S. Eliot memorably castigated as 'living and partly living.'

Curiosity and comedy - science and literature: these 'are not two things: they are two aspects of the same thing' - so wrote T.H. Huxley: and what terrible errors we might have avoided if we had based our political, educational and social behaviour on this understanding! Not two cultures, but one culture in two aspects.

II

Can we then take this image of Life as a *Dance to the Music of Time* and explore it for such insight as it may open up for us towards a better understanding of who we are and what we are to do? 'Who am I? What are my gifts, abilities, limitations; what are my hopes, my fears? Being such a person as this, what am I meant to be doing with my life? To which of all the harmonies and discords I hear around me - the music of our times - should I listen and dance?'

Curiosity and comedy are convenient probes with which to explore our immediate environment, the experience of a university. For a few years we have each been given to each other in this context. Time's music to which we are invited to dance in this academic season of our human quest - holding hands but facing outwards - time's music plays for the exercise of our imagination, of our intellect, of our feeling. As feeling person to feeling person we observe, explore, relate to each other, approaching, withdrawing, testing ourselves in a quite new, sometimes exhilarating sometimes frightening movement of possible relationships and possible rejections. As questioning minds to questioning minds we give freer range to our intellectual curiosity than we did at school: the desire to know - to get to the bottom of things - to find out for ourselves - to form our own opinions; and to do this whatever the immediate subject-matter of our enquiry, be it mathematics, or philosophy, or Latin American literature. But if in all this interplay of minds and persons there is no development of the sensibilities of imagination, then what does it profit a man if he gains the whole world of learning and is a social success but forfeits his own soul? Charles Morgan was surely right when he said there is no such thing as failure except failure of imagination.

III

But whether older or younger, newcomers or old-hands, beneath and around and beyond our immediate academic and administrative tasks is always our consciousness of ourselves, awareness of our human nature, human condition, human predicament. Those of us who move towards retirement and old age find ourselves asking different questions, facing different uncertainties from those of you for whom the future lies open with all its unknown latent possibilities of danger and delight. Politically, economically, socially, internationally we are all caught up in the convulsions and uncertainties of old systems that are dying and new systems that are labouring to be born. But personally, individually, humanly in the silence and solitude of our own hearts there are the same human questions and doubts which men and women have wrestled with since the dawn of human self-consciousness; questions and searchings which exercise poets and novelists and philosophers and theologians: questionings which for much of the time we suppress until they erupt through the protective casing of our reluctance and force us to decide.

There have been periods in past times in which there has been a generally accepted view about the meaning of things - a framework of beliefs and rules within which a person could live with some degree of confidence. Myths are stories men of old told themselves as a way of controlling and organising feeling, thought, action. And even today when, as T.S. Eliot has put it, we 'know only a heap of broken images,' the ancient myths continue to be catalysts for many modern poets. Edwin Muir's poetry moves with equal assurance from Greek myths and Christian myths in the confidence that these ancient insights - if re-presented - can not only stir sub-conscious memories, but actually lead us in the confusion and disorder of these times 'to the point where it is possible for us to make a rational and moral choice.' (W.H. Auden).

I would feel I had not detained you unprofitably if as a result I had encouraged more of you to spend more time with the poets. I urge this not only because the poets explore the possibilities of language and extend its significance: I urge this also because so much of the language of Christianity has the character of poetry, of metaphor, or symbol. To fail to recognise this is to fail to perceive true meanings.

In our present open, pluralist culture in which there is no common code, no clear directives, no obvious and acknowledged purpose, I believe we are being forced back to explore afresh quite basic assumptions and experiences, and to discover in a new simplicity what we may hope and what we should do. Eliot has it again, and with no apology:

> We shall not cease from exploration
> And the end of all our exploring
> Will be to arrive where we started
> And know the place for the first time.

IV

The basic question is, I believe, this: Can reality be trusted?

As a matter of fact every human being every day lives in attitudes of trust. We couldn't survive otherwise. To act you must assume and that assumption is faith. We put confidence in the reliability of things, in the trustworthiness of people. Every day we run the risk of putting confidence in people and in things we can't control. Sometimes our acts of trust are total as when in a hospital we hand ourselves over to the anaesthetist and the surgeon. Everything depends on the reliability of the thing, the trustworthiness of the person. Trust means reliance: reliance involves risk. Can we take this unavoidable element of risk in human life to the point of ultimate trust? Can we rely on reality as trustworthy all along the line? Can we believe in God? For I take it that belief in God is a way of expressing trust in the ultimate reliability of the human experiment.

I said this was the basic human question: I also believe it to be the question at the base of our more immediate contemporary malaise. People today seem to be less willing to trust other people: other people are becoming less worthy of trust. People are less willing to trust institutions, processes of law, governments, authorities of any kind. And perhaps authorities are becoming less worthy of trust. If there is no trust in an ultimate authority as true and reliable and good, it seems that there is a lessening of trustworthiness right through society. If life is thought to be capricious, futile, absurd: if I'm answerable to nobody, why should I bother?

Even those of us who do believe that reality is to be trusted, even those of us who do open our lives in faith and hope and love to that God whom Jesus addressed in the total trustingness expressed in his *Abba: Father*, we too in these confused and confusing days often feel ourselves poised precariously over an abyss of questioning doubt. Yes! we know that there can be no such thing as faith which does not contain within itself essential doubt. We can't trust another without risk. The anaesthetist, weary from long hours in the operating theatre, may turn the wrong knob at the critical moment. Men and women of faith inevitably carry within themselves as part of themselves something of the godlessness and bafflement of the times in which we are living. Can then the Christian affirmations about God, about Christ, about new life in the Spirit any longer claim our allegiance and our trust?

The fact is that the Christian affirmations about God: Father, Son and Holy Spirit, and the life that follows from these affirmations do continue to claim the allegiance and the trust of millions of men and women. Statistics of church-going are no measure of the persistence of faith, or the practice of prayer, or the exercise of love. The Christ kind of loving is kept in circulation along a multitude of hidden arteries.

If you wonder what power sustains that marvellous woman Mother Teresa and others like her in their daily costly caring for the thousands of homeless poor people in Calcutta, you won't find the answer in 'social conscience' or 'human compassion'. She is sustained by her amazing faith in the love of God for herself and for the suffering ones whose needs she can hardly begin to touch. 'I can only do what I can' - she said when asked if she was not overwhelmed by the immensity of the task.

Christianity in our times is discarding old forms and seeking new forms. Try to encapsulate Christianity in a stereotype and sooner or later it will break the capsule. Our westernised way of doing theology has become highly specialised, far removed from the experience of ordinary people, hardly affected by the social and political upheavals, the shifts of power, the struggles for freedom. But in Latin America by contrast Christians insist that talk about God, talk about the Christian interpretation of life must arise out of actual lived experience: and experience for them is the experience of being politically oppressed and economically exploited.

But even in our tired European world, Christianity is neither dead nor dying. Sloughing off old skins is easier for snakes than for societies. But change is our condition. 'The faith and trust of the heart,' wrote Martin Luther, 'makes both God and idol.' Not all change is change towards clearer perception of truth; but to refuse to change is to refuse to live. If we are to live we must change - not by discarding tradition but by allowing tradition to be the seedbed of new creations. A false desire for the false security of a false authority has all too often bedevilled the life of the Spirit. But if we will listen attentively to the secret harmonies of the past we shall find ourselves able to dance to the music of Christ with a new freedom, a recovered spontaneity.

With the drawing of this Love and the voice of this
Calling . . .
. . . all shall be well and
All manner of thing shall be well.
By the purification of the motive
In the ground of our beseeching.

Yes! the purification of the motive and the simplification of
the style.

V

'What then shall we do, you and I?' 'What are the alternatives?' 'The alternatives are to drift or to decide'. 'To decide
what?' 'To decide to dance and not to drift. 'And if I decide to
dance, to what music shall I respond?'

If you are to be a real person, the person you are capable
of becoming, a vibrant, animated, loving person, a person
other people will come to trust, you must first become clear
about where *you* are going to put *your own* trust. What others
find you to be will in fact be what you really are: and what you
really are is all bound up with what you set your heart on in the
last resort. A human person reflects what he sets his heart on.
But there's some headwork to be done first. You need to be
sure enough of the reliability of what you're going to set your
heart on. One question you will ask yourself is what sort of a
person you want to become; what sort of a person you want
others to find you to be; what sort of a person you want your
children in future years to find you to be. This is a tremen-
dously important choice. The way we are with others reflects
the way we are within ourselves: the way we are within
ourselves reflects the way we are with God. A human person
reflects what he set his heart on. *So* - 'will you, won't you, will
you, won't you, will you join the dance?'

'But how can I be sure?' 'Sure of what?' 'Sure that all will
be well'. 'You can only be sure by getting into the dance and
letting the leader of the dance teach you the steps'. Only in the
dance to the music and choreography of Christ shall we be
able to give to God such total trust as is conveyed by words of

85

Prisoners of Hope

Florizel to Perdita in Shakespeare's *Winter's Tale*:
> ... I cannot be
> Mine own, nor anything to any, if
> I be not thine.

To be a Priest

What is a priest for?

The short answer is that he is a man for God and a man for others. He is a man for God and a man for others in the sort of way that Jesus was a man for God and a man for others. And the special sphere from which he operates is the sphere of the Christian community which is both universal in range and local in expression.

In what way then is a deacon or a priest different from every other man or woman who belongs to the Christian community? Should we not say of every baptised Christian that he, that she, is for God and for others in the sort of way that Jesus was for God and for others? Certainly we should say that. Whatever else a deacon or a priest is, he is basically an ordinary member of the Christian community, committed as all Christians are to order his life for God and for others.

What else then is a priest or a deacon?

He is a man who accepts responsibilities over and above the responsibilities he has already accepted as a baptised Christian. He is a man on whom the Church lays responsibilities over and above the responsibilities which the Church lays on all her members. All that Christ is towards God and towards others; all that the Church is towards God and towards others; all that the lay Christian is towards God and towards others: all this is as it were focused, accentuated, brought out into relief in what a priest is.

A priest is a lay Christian set apart by vocation and training and ordination to accentuate - by what he is - what the Church is and what the Gospel is. I find this idea of priesthood as a focus - as an accentuation of what is true of the Church and of the Gospel - helps me to see both the priesthood of all believers and the priesthood of priests in their mutuality and in their distinction.

Equally a priest is a man set apart in order to spend his time, his energy, his abilities, his understanding and his love in helping the Christian community to become more obviously and genuinely what it is intended to be. He is both a *sign* of what the Church is and an *instrument* within the Church for helping the Church actually to become more effectively and more relevantly what it already is. By his presence and by his person he exists to help the local congregation become more genuinely and more committedly a community of people who live not for themselves but for God and for other people. As Archbishop William Temple never tired of saying: 'The Church in this world exists for the sake of those who are outside it.'

If the Church in every neighbourhood is to go on growing into a body of people who keep love in circulation by being the kind of people they are, then each local congregation needs spiritual leadership, needs constant reminders of what the Church and the Christian is meant to be, needs someone in their midst to keep fresh their vision, and keep strong their desire to order their lives for God and for others in the sort of way that Jesus lived. The local community needs a ministry of word and sacrament.

Sometimes men say that they can serve the community as Christians better by being out in the world's life as lay persons than by being ordained. The fallacy in this statement lies in the implied comparison. There is no question that Christian lay men can and do and must serve their fellows in a Christian direction by the way they live and work in their particular trade or business. But this is not a 'better' way; it is a different way; and the way of the priest is the way of serving those who are to offer a lay service in ordinary secular occupations. The priest is needed to help the lay Church to become a local centre of faith and prayer and commitment giving strength and support to the individuals who are trying to live a Christian life in the life of the world. The lay Christian needs the priest and the priest needs the lay Christian. There needs to be a mutual recognition and a reciprocity of love between Christian people and those who serve the Christian people as deacons and as priests. Theirs is a shared ministry - two aspects of the single ministry which is Christ in the Church and the Church in the world.

The separation of the priest is precisely in order that the priest may become more involved. He is a man set apart in order that he may be set within his local congregation in a way which accentuates what the Church is for and serves the Church towards becoming more genuinely what it is. He is separated out from the whole body of Christians - a marked man - in order that he may become more totally committed to the whole body of Christians as their servant. He is paid to be free - paid to be accessible - paid to be totally involved.

II

And what is this priestly service? Is it not a service directed towards the growth in all who will respond to a new quality of personal living? Is it not a service directed towards the liberation in men and women of their full potentialities for personalness, for understanding, for out-going love to God and to others?

The educational services of the State will have this as their aim up to a point. The enlarging of people's awareness of the world in which they live, of the treasures of literature and music and art; the training of minds to think correctly and the encouragement of creativities of head and hand; the experience of being in touch with other persons and with other minds - this whole enterprise of education will result in a growth of personal being. And along various channels of culture will come a knowledge of Christ and the Christian virtues. Christian influences making for more sensitive personal self-awareness and self-giving to others are not by any means confined to the special agencies of communication in a parish. This we should recognise and welcome and work with; and especially with those teachers in schools and colleges who see in their teaching something more than the giving of information, who see their teaching as an opportunity for helping persons to develop as persons. Learning for living.

But the strengthening of the educational services of the State by securing a supply of teachers who have this larger Christian and more personal understanding of education calls for the constant presence of the more committed community of Christians with their priest at the centre keeping fresh and clear that vision of what it means to be a person - which is the vision of Christ as the man for God and the man for others.

A priest of the Church has among other tasks that of becoming an *interpreter*, interpreting people to themselves; interpreting people to each other; interpreting the movements of the times in which we live; interpreting all this in relation to that unveiling of meaning which is God's self-revelation in Christ. This necessary and continuing work of interpretation requires of us a life-long habit of reading and reflection, of observation and appraisal. And it is by becoming this kind of person in our early years that we shall keep open our growth into a wiser, loving and a maturer understanding in our later years.

If one function of the priest is to be an *interpreter*, another function is to be an *enabler* - a person who by virtue of his own understanding can enable others to cope with the particular demands of their own experience and to grow as persons through the way they learn to cope. Call this counselling; call this spiritual direction; call it what you will, this work of enabling persons to grow into better persons is a priestly work for which there is an ever growing need; even if the need is often as yet unrecognised; even if the priest is not always seen as the man whose faith and whose training and whose understanding makes him the man for others at this level. Prepare yourself each year to become a more effective enabler as you grow older.

To be among people as a man who is known and trusted and used - this should be one of your desires for yourself as a priest - to be an enabler - and able to be an enabler because you have experienced such help yourself from others.

Now to be at people's service at this level - to be accessible, to be open, to be able to listen, to be wise - this is something for which we have to be patient in preparing ourselves. This kind of service of others is a different sort of service from that of the doctor or the psychiatric social worker or the child care officer or the schoolteacher. It touches their service at many points. Priests have much they can learn about human nature and the experience of being human from such experts as those I have mentioned. But the priestly service, the service of others in the dimension of faith - the service of others that is sustained by a vision of their latent capacities for growth as persons - this kind of service belongs to the Christian community as such and to the priests of the community in particular.

To be among people as such a man, open and available, is to live in one sense a very unstructured sort of life. And this calls for a degree of spiritual and emotional maturity - a confidence and a conviction based on experience. Into such a confidence we each have to grow; and this takes time; and we must be patient. But all the time we can keep before us this desire - to become this kind of priest - for God and for others, at this level of interpreter and enabler.

It is at this level that we are at one with our Lord in whose life and teaching and relationships with people we see focused and accentuated and brought into relief the age-long presence and providence of God as reconciler and sanctifier.

III

Behind the priesthood of the priest is the priesthood of the Church; behind the priesthood of the Church is the priesthood of Christ; and the priesthood of Christ is the presence of God as reconciler and sanctifier - the presence of God bringing his creation to perfection by the costly process of enabling his creatures freely to choose their perfection and to follow it.

For every man and woman there is the possibility of their individual personal fulfilment and growth towards perfection; not some abstract perfection, but the particular perfection of each particular person, a perfection compounded of his personality and his circumstances and of the way in which he has learned how to bring his temperament and this situation into a life directed towards God and towards others.

As interpreters and as enablers we who are priests are

agents of the reconciling and sanctifying presence and power of God who desires that all men and women shall become through Christ all that they have it in them to become. To be at the service of others for the development of their latent potential towards the high possibilities of personal fulfilment in Christ - this is what it means to be a priest - this is what our ministry of interpreting and enabling is all about. Keep this always before you as your reason for being a priest. Keep this always before you whatever the difficulties and the frustrations you experience on the institutional side of the Church's life.

And let this ministry of interpretation and enablement be the standard by which you criticise and seek to change the inherited patterns of Church practice in the years ahead. Reform there must be. I doubt if our would-be reformers are radical enough; and if they are not radical enough it is because they are not approaching reform with a sufficiently penetrating theological appraisal of what the Church is for. But you will be the reformers of the Church in the next forty years. Let your critiques and therefore your reforms be rooted in a radical understanding of what the Gospel is, of what the Church is, of what the Church and the ministry exist to do for men and women. Let reform be always towards a better interpretation and a better enablement - towards the evoking of the high possibilities of individual persons each towards his and her individual perfection through a life lived for God and for others.

IV

Your ability to do this - to be an interpreter and an enabler - will be effective in so far as you are living your own life by the insights of the Gospel, in so far as you are allowing yourselves to be made what you are by the Gospel you preach.

This means that you will be seeing every suffering that comes to you, every difficulty and frustration, every failure and disappointment, as so much raw material for your growth in holiness. Everything is grist to the mill for the man who sees this as the secret of the Christian life. There is a way of interiorising all our sufferings so that they are accepted and made into ever deepening commitment to God and to others. Often you will find that the raw material of your praying will be the problems and the frustrations of trying to be an interpreter and enabler, and feeling inadequate and ineffective. But this is to live the life of a priest on its most interior side; and it is in this way that true priests are made. We cannot place ourselves on the side of love in its encounter with all that is not love without being made to suffer. But in Christ we have seen that there is a kind of loving which is indestructible - for all that evil can do to this kind of loving is to give this love ever-fresh opportunities of loving.

What it means to be a priest at this level you will have to discover for yourselves. But my prayer for you as you approach ordination is that you will allow yourselves to discover what it means to be a priest at this level; for then you will discover what I also pray you will all discover - and that is the joy of being a priest.

Heaven upon Earth

I

On 31 August, 1826, a certain traveller made this entry in his diary:

'Yesterday morning I went into the Cathedral at Salisbury about 7 o'clock. When I got into the nave of the Church and was looking up and admiring the columns and the roof I heard a sort of *humming* in some place which appeared to be in the transept of the building. I wondered what it was, and made my way towards the place whence the noise appeared to issue. As I approached the noise seemed to grow louder. At last I thought I could distinguish the sounds of a human voice. This encouraged me to proceed: and still following the sound I at last turned in at a doorway to my left where I found a priest and his congregation assembled. It was a parson of some sort, with a white covering on him, and five women and four men. I joined the congregation until they came to the Litany: and then being monstrously hungry I did not think myself bound to stay any longer. I wonder what the founders would say, if they could rise from the grave and see such a congregation as this in this most magnificent and beautiful Cathedral.'

If William Cobbett were rurally riding into the Cathedral *this* morning, he might indeed have *wondered* what the founders would say ... but *this* morning even his sardonic detachment would have taken on overtones of amazement and joy.

How different in spirit was George Herbert, the poet priest of neighbouring Bemerton, of whom Izaak Walton wrote:

' ... though he was a lover of retiredness, yet his love to Musick was such that he went usually twice every week on certain appointed days to the Cathedral Church in Salisbury: and at his return would say that his time spent

94

in Prayer and Cathedral Musick elevated his soul, and was his Heaven upon Earth.'

II

'Ought you not', asked the young girl in a visiting group of sixth-formers to whom a few days ago I was speaking about the liturgical heart-beat of a cathedral's inner life, 'ought you not', she said, 'to give all this up and hand over the money to help refugees?'

I replied that I too rarely went through a day without thinking of the Indo-Chinese boat people and all the other forgotten homeless people whose plight no longer reaches the headlines. I said that I hoped that the City of Salisbury, and in this audience, may I add, perhaps the citizens of Winchester and Chichester as well, will be wanting to receive some of these bright, civilised and hard-working Indo-Chinese to come and make a new life for themselves with us. Then I went on to try to help this compassionate young adult to see that a cathedral stands for a deeper truth no less important for human well-being than the meeting of the immediate deprivations and needs of homeless refugees, a truth which goes to the roots of man's inhumanity to man.

And as I spoke I found myself remembering the episode in the house of Simon the Leper when the unnamed woman poured on the head of Jesus the whole content of an alabaster jar of very expensive ointment. The indignant disciples protested: 'Why this waste? The ointment might have been sold for a large sum and given to the poor.' To which Jesus responded with one of his hard and enigmatic sayings: 'Why do you trouble the woman? She has done a beautiful thing for me. You always have the poor with you: but you do not always have me.'

If the Southern Cathedrals Festival were to have a patron of the patrons surely it should be this woman. Not at all forgetting the poor and the terrible hurts that are being done every hour of every day by some human persons to other human persons, we dare to pour out our alabaster jars of precious ointment in that most wasteful of all effusions - the effusion of worship. We dare in this century of appalling human acts of brutality and shame to do what by the utilitarian valuations of the secular mind are acts which are totally useless. Useless yes! but not empty! For if this torturing twentieth century has taught us anything, it has taught us the truth of Berdyaev's word: 'Where there is no God, there is no man'.

Worship is man's supreme affirmation of God and therefore of his own true nature. To worship God we must pour ourselves out with the lavish generosity of the unnamed woman in the house of Simon the Leper whose glorious wastefulness earned from Jesus the recognition of the inward heart-meaning of her act: 'Truly I say to you, wherever this Gospel is preached in the whole world, what she has done will be told in memory to her.'

This kneeling, this singing, this reading from ancient
    books,
This acknowledgement that the burden is intolerable, this
    promise of amendment,
This humble access, this putting out of the hands,
This taking of the bread and wine, this returning to your
    place not glancing about you,
This solemn acceptance and the thousand sins that will
    follow it,
This thousand sins and the repenting of them,
This dedication and this apostasy, this apostasy and this
    restoration,
This thousand restorations and this thousand apostasies,
Take and accept them all, be not affronted nor dismayed
    by them.
They are a net of holes to capture essence, a shell to house
    the thunder of an ocean,
A discipline of petty acts to catch Creation, a rune of
    words to hold one Living Word,
A ladder built by men of sticks and stones, whereby they
    hope to reach to heaven.

So wrote the South African, Alan Paton, in a poem for his godson at his confirmation. George Herbert found in the worship of the Cathedral 'his heaven upon earth'. The ladder is the ladder of Jacob's dream - with angels of God ascending and descending upon it. That tremendous Lover, the Hound of Heaven in Francis Thompson's imagination, came down from heaven to take us into heaven: heaven here and heaven hereafter. The Divine Beauty visits time but belongs to eternity.

III

Do we perhaps hesitate to speak of beauty in the same breath in which we speak the name of God? Fearful puritans and angry iconoclasts see the form of beauty only as the shape of an idol. Again George Herbert comes to our rescue:

A man that looks on glass

On it may stay his eye;

Or, if he pleaseth, through it pass,

And then the heaven espy.

We can't do without this word Beauty, in life or in the things of the spirit. Beauty is the only word which describes an experience that appeals at once to the imagination and to the senses. Without intellect we would not be human: but the reasons of the heart and the explorations of the imagination alone can make and keep us truly human. What any individual finds beautiful may change at different periods of his or her life. The most beautiful tune ceases to rouse a response in the listener if he hears it played too often: but in another sense, sensibility to beauty is indestructible. The ear, even if tired of one tune too often repeated, is always ready to respond freely to another. The beauty we find in the creative arts is surely a beauty that *finds us* - and what else can true beauty be but a visit from the beauty that is a radiance of God.

Shall we then receive as a gift from the beyond mediated to us in the here and now this cascade of musical melody and rhythm? Shall we let it flow into us and through us and become within us the energy of our loving response to the tremendous Lover, at once so aweful and so accessible whose joy is our response?

We aren't here as listeners to a concert: we're here to break the alabaster jar of our hearts' deepest longing for someone to adore. Worship is an effusion of gratitude, recognition, joy. Music is one of God's gifts to take us beyond ourselves into the presence of that adorable Mystery, 'in whom we live and move and have our being', to that Beauty 'both so ancient and so new' - 'who is and who was and who is to come'.

The Lord's Song in a Strange Land

I

The land that is strange is our own land, our whole world that has become strange to us. Our song sounds strange in the ears of our contemporaries. How shall we sing our Lord's strange song in a world that has become strange to us as we have become strange to it?

Never before has the entire human race been poised so precariously on the edge - of what? Disaster or new disclosure? Predictive analysts of the future base their doom-laden warnings on what they extrapolate from trends they discern in present time: relentless pressure of escalating population: shortages of food and energy: the frightening stock-pile of thermonuclear destructiveness: the uncontrolled momentum of science and technology; political inertia; individual blindness. Great powers feed each other's fears. No national government is wholly in control of its affairs. Economically, politically, strategically, intelligent and dedicated men and women work at the problems but no way forward claims conviction. Unemployment continues to rise and no one who lived in County Durham as I did for most of the years 1934-43 can be under any illusion about the damage to human persons and families that results from long-term unemployment.

What the doom-writers can't identify, however, are those more hidden, counteravailing energies that are also and always at work in human society changing attitudes, opening up new possibilities. Things may fall apart, but the Centre of all centres does in fact hold. Signals of hope shine less brightly, but we who profess and call ourselves Christians are by the fact of our faith prisoners of hope; pledged to seek always the counteravailing energies that make for creative solutions; pledged always to take our stand within those energies at the point where love and evil meet; pledged to stand with Christ crucified and risen.

99

Disaster or new discovery? Which will it be? But what is there left for mankind to discover? The exterior universe has been explored and mapped with radio-telescope and electron microscope. We've seen our planet earth photographed by men on their way to the moon. What Copernicus and Galileo began, today's astronauts and astronomers, biologists and chemists have completed. We've reached the end of Renaissance Man.

Yet still in spite of our knowledge and our powers, we remain a mystery to ourselves and a problem to each other. What is there left for modern man to discover? We have yet to discover how to live with each other, person with person, group with group. In a situation in which an old world struggles to survive and a new world struggles to be born, we in Britain have to discover how to live and play together in this painful post-imperial, post-industrial era, when traditional labour requirements are coming to an end and new electronic processes are leaving more and more men and women with unorganised time on their hands and gnawing anxiety in their hearts.

The Synod is appointed to serve the Christian community in order that the local communities of Christians in villages and towns and cities shall be encouraged and assisted to communicate the truth that is in Christ Jesus and to liberate the love of God in every neighbourhood. Much of the Synod's time will be taken up with unavoidable domestic decisions in aid of good house-keeping. We are the guardians of an inheritance and managers of an institution. But the institution exists not to perpetuate itself but to propagate a gospel. 'What we preach is not ourselves, but Jesus Christ as Lord, with ourselves as your servants for Jesus' sake.'

II

If you walk up towards Marble Arch from Hyde Park Corner, you will see on your left on a mound of grass on the edge of the Park a cluster of bronze shapes. These sculptures are the last big work of Barbara Hepworth. She called these bronzes *The Family of Man*: ancestors, parents, children, newly-weds -

and just beyond them the figure she called *Ultimate Form*. I don't know to whose imagination and gift we owe the presence of this symbolic affirmation of the primacy of the personal set among the swirling traffic of this hurrying city. One World: One People: One Human Family. To this larger vision we are being urged to respond by both the discoveries and the disasters that distinguish this our time. No longer can place be found for tribalisms, racialisms, sectarianisms, fundamentalisms. What God would seem to be saying in and through the turbulence and the tragedies is that we must all learn to acknowledge and accept each other across old barriers and explore new ways of living together without losing what is distinctive and humanly good in our different cultures. Within this movement towards universal ecumenism can we doubt that the international experience of the communities of Christians has a special contribution to make?

III

But all around us are men and women of goodwill who have long ceased to expect from the Church any meaningful guidelines for their human journey. The issue of belief and unbelief affects us all. There is a would-be believer in every unbeliever; an agnostic in every church-goer. Belief and agnosticism are not incompatible. Faith is not certainty but a willingness to explore; doubt is not a rejection of faith but an honest refusal to be prematurely persuaded. Christianity is an offered answer to the human quest for meaning; an invitation to explore life in the light of the Christian interpretation. If this Synod is to serve the Church and if the Church is to serve the people among whom we live at this deep level of uncertainty and need and search, then this Synod in and through all it does must bend its endeavours to help the local communities of Christians to make Christianity visible, to make Christianity intelligible, to make Christianity desirable.

(i) To make Christianity visible: that is to help men and women to see it as a really possible way of looking at things. There is work here for artists and poets and playwrights; for musicians, journalists, broadcasters. Every day now, in our

Cathedral at Salisbury, I see people sitting down to contemplate Gabriel Loire's superb new east window that sets Christ crucified in relation to prisoners of conscience of the twentieth century. Some of them write to me. They've been enabled to see the point and make new connections.

But making Christianity visible - a really possible way of understanding and responding to life as it comes - is no less the task of local Christian congregations in their relationships with each other and with their neighbours. The new shape of the Eucharistic liturgy in the Alternative Service Book does unquestionably stimulate a new experience of togetherness in Christ, a more visible expression of the new possibilities in relationships which is a Christ-gift to human persons.

(ii) Secondly, our endeavour must be to make Christianity intelligible to our contemporaries. There is work enough here for our theologians: work enough for those who prepare study courses for lay men and women in the dioceses; work enough for Christian teachers in colleges and schools. Most urgent for this Synod, because long overdue, is a new initiative in this crucial area of the moral and religious education of the young. What is needed is massive and imaginative endeavour on the part of the Church.

Our Anglican understanding of Christian truth has never been fossilised in dogmatic formulas. We've understood Christian truth as living, dynamic, given and yet always to be discovered afresh by the guiding of the Holy Spirit provided we will keep our minds actively engaged in the threefold dialectic of scripture, tradition and reason. The certitudes of faith require the exercise of self-giving love as well as the exercise of thought. Those who do the will shall know the doctrine. But all this needs to be rethought and restated in the altogether different intellectual and social climate of our times. We must be open to the questions: 'What do you mean?' and 'How do you know?' But we shall also do well to remember one sentence from the now forgotten book published in 1945 by an Archbishop's Commission with the brave title: *Towards the Conversion of England*. The sentence runs:

Ultimately the evidence for the credibility of the Gospel in the eyes of the world will rest upon the evidence of a quality of life in the Church which the world cannot find elsewhere.

(iii) Thirdly, our endeavour must be so to present Christianity that men and women and boys and girls shall find it desirable. This third task requires that we discover and draw out those impulses in every person which the Gospel is given to satisfy so that the relevance and the excellence of it may be felt. So often our failure to attract the interest of our contemporaries is due to our failure to understand them. What we are so often lacks the joyfulness and the glory of a truly Christian holy humanness.

The essence of Christianity is offering - the deep offering of ourselves, our souls and bodies: to the sign and sacrament of this offering we now turn in this Eucharist, acting in God's eye what in God's eye we are:

Christ - for Christ plays in ten thousand places,
Lovely in limbs, and lovely in eyes not his
To the Father through the features of men's faces.

Companions of the Way

I

On our journey through life we each know what it is to be alone - to feel alone - to experience the reality of our essential personal solitude: in moments of fear, or when we alone have to make a difficult decision; or when we reflect deeply on the mystery of life and ask ultimate questions. Perhaps you can remember that moment of panic when you were a child out with your parents when there were crowds of other people about; something attracted your attention; and then suddenly you realised that your parents weren't there, they'd moved on thinking that you were following; you were very small; those other people were so big; you couldn't see your parents. Or, if you have no recollection of this for yourself, you've probably seen a child in panic tears who feels itself lost being out of sight of the safety and security that parents represent and indeed effect.

Or later in life when you reflect on your existence, it really dawns on you that one day you will die. 'I am' and 'I am to die.' A new seriousness is reached when you realise the inevitability of the 'I am to die.' You understand that your life journey is only as long as the distance between 'I am' and 'I am to die.'

As part of our inner equipment for the journey, we each know and need to know what it is to be be alone, to feel alone; to experience desolation, perhaps on being suddenly taken very ill and finding yourself coming round from the operation. But even more important for our inner equipment for the journey, we need to know that we are not alone; there are always others. With these others we have differing kinds of relationship, differing degrees of intimacy, of indifference, of hostility. Sometime we find in the companionship of others feelings of joy and support; sometimes feelings of irritation;

sometimes the sense of being under-valued, rejected, ignored, passed over. But it is well to remember that 'we owe our genuinely personal existence as much to our enemies as to our friends'; to those who criticise us as much as to those who are sympathetic, encouraging and helpful. Antagonism can stimulate the growth in us of inner awareness and resources that keep us alive, whereas comfortable people allow us to drift and atrophy.

Sometimes on our journey we experience aloneness; but for the most part we journey with companions - some of whom we like; some of whom we dislike. Alone, we are not alone.

II

What does our Christian faith contribute to our ability to relate to those who at any time are our given companions on the journey? 'Hell,' wrote Jean Paul Sartre, 'hell is other people.' 'Hell,' wrote T.S. Eliot, 'hell is oneself.' Our Christianity says of Jesus that 'he descended into hell.' What that refers to is the coming of the crucified Jesus into the abode of the departed as envisaged in the Hebrew and early Christian imagination. I am taking 'hell' to mean what Sartre and Eliot were meaning. And let's take 'heaven' to mean what many a popular song-lyric uses the word to mean - relationships full of love and delight. Heaven and hell are words that in this use stand for different poles of our experience of the presence with us of others on the journey of life and of our own inner state.

The supreme contribution of Christianity to our experience of being alone and of being not alone is the conviction that, however we feel and whatever we experience, the whole journey is being made in the company of one who is beyond time and space and yet within time and space. God is the 'beyond in our midst.' It is in God that we 'live and move and have our being.' God is as much the companion of our nights and days as is the air we breathe and the oxygen that enables us to live.

III

One of the obstacles in the way of faith and prayer is the vagueness of our ideas of God. I venture to speak of God under the image of a *dimension*, such as the dimensions of space and time, only more dynamic, more personally experienced. God is a real dimension of the life everybody is already living. God is, whether we acknowledge God or not.

What our Christianity does is to help us to think of the unthinkable in personal terms. We are encouraged to think of God as personal presence, as personal claim. What Jesus offers us is the experience of God in a relationship of faith. Jesus expresses this relationship in terms of Father and Son. But in order that our human experience of father and son shall work as the basis for us of a sense of God, the human relationship has to be disinfected of all that would make the analogy work against it as a basis. For Edmund Gosse, his experience of being a son of his actual father was far removed from the relationship that Jesus taught and practised. God as Father: yes! but what sort of a father; and ourself what sort of a son? I always remember a young offender in prison who said he had no objection to being required to attend services of worship in the prison chapel. 'But I won't say *Our Father*: my father's a bastard.' Our personal experience of being a son, of being a daughter, can vary from love to hate, from joy to disgust. At best it can act as an indication of the way to a sense of God; at worst the experience is distorting and destructive; and yet even this can lead the victim to imagine a father and son relationship that is of a different quality and open up a hope.

Our human relationship, then, has to be purified of some of what it contains before it can be used as the foundation of our relationship with God. But there's enough in the experience of most of us to enable it to be transposed. The Gospel story of Jesus helps us to make this transposition. 'No man has seen God at any time; the only begotten who is in the bosom of the Father, he has declared him.' So writes St John. 'He that has seen me has seen the Father', says Jesus in the Fourth Gospel: as if he was saying, 'Learn what sort of a father God is by observing how I relate to him'. Jesus lived in a conscious awareness of God as presence, as claim, as companion, as Father. Can you and I reach a clearer picture of God by contemplating what is revealed of his character in the way Jesus spoke of him, related to him? What we need is not a visual image, but a set of attitudes and responses. We need to discern the 'behaviour patterns' that underlie the Gospel stories. To live in the sense of God as present, of God as companion of the journey means to become aware of God as a loving presence who makes demands for our good but never demands the impossible: to become aware of God as one who knows all there is to be known about oneself, but as one who nevertheless accepts and forgives; to become aware of God as one who in every situation wants us to see the truth and to see the error so that we can return from the error back to the truth; so that wrong-doing and bad feeling can be transmuted by forgiveness into a growth-point for progress towards greater good: *this* is the Christian vocation.

I said a moment ago that what we need is not a visual image. But sometimes a visual image can help. Millions of Christians have been helped by the visual image of the helplessness of the crucified Jesus, understood as the expression in time and space of the lengths to which Divine Love will go for the sake of his love for us and our true life. An image that has helped me as much as any other is a carving of Christ crucified by the sculptor Jagger which once stood on the rood screen of the chapel of the Society of the Sacred Mission at Kelham. The face is the face of a living man; his head crowned with thorns. The eyes are open and they look deep into one's soul with infinite seriousness and infinite mercy. The look is one that won't allow one to pretend, or evade the truth about oneself. The look is stern - but if you don't turn your eyes away from the sternness, you discover that the look is the look of a stern *love*. Love predominates; but there's no avoiding the conclusion: 'If you love me, you will keep my commandments.' The severity is the depth of the love. The love is such that it will not let us go until we have given up all pretence, insincerity, evasion, dishonesty, false pride; until we have surrendered all, so that he may set us free and give us our true self in exchange. His sculpture always reminds me of Francis

Thompson's poem *The Hound of Heaven* with those haunting sentences:

> All things betray thee who betrayest Me
> Naught shelters thee, who wilt not shelter Me
> Lo! naught contents thee, who content'st not Me
> Lo! all things fly thee, for thou fliest me
> Thou dravest love from thee, who dravest Me.

IV

Such is the unseen companion of our journey; such is the sublime gift of Jesus to the world; the supreme contribution of Christianity to our human understanding. This is the truth that shall make us free. And it is this truth that claims us all along the route, opening up for us new life in the discovery of sacrificial love. All this accompanies us if we allow ourselves to believe in the reality of the communion of saints; saints of old we can read about; and saints of our own time whose quality we begin to discern once we ourselves have begun to give up false values and false aims and are surrendering to the love of God.

May I remind you of what Pierre de Caussade said about the hiddenness of the inner riches of understanding and caring in those who have embraced the way of self-abandonment. Such hidden riches are to be glimpsed in many unlikely places, in many unexpected faces, in many surprises of insight, word, gesture - a look in the eyes, the touch of a hand. Do you know the poem by Richard Baxter?

> He wants not friends that hath thy love,
> And may converse and walk with thee:
> And with thy saints here and above
> With whom for ever I must be.
> In the communion of saints
> Is wisdom, safety and delight:
> And when my heart declines and faints
> It's raised by their heat and light.

The Christian community of faith on its most interior side is just such a hidden companionship of men and women who have long abandoned the false values of superficial aims and ambitions, all bitterness and superficiality; men and women who have learned that the good life is life lived for God and for other people. The choice Christ invites us to make is the crucial naked choice for or against sacrificial loving as the law of life. The Christian community exists to keep such love in circulation in a world full of evil and destructiveness, but full too of inexhaustible possibilities of growth in love. Such love is gloriously in circulation within the communities of Christians, but not all that is in circulation within any Christian community is yet love. Not all is yet love.

You know that. But does that knowledge grieve you? Ought it not to grieve us that not all that circulates amongst us is yet the Christ kind of loving? What then shall we do? We must repent. We must believe. We must pray.

V

i. We must repent. Only if we repent shall we be humble. Only if we are humble shall we be willing to listen. Only if we listen to one another shall we really love.

ii. We must believe. What makes a man or a woman what each is, is the set of assumptions on which they habitually think, on which they habitually act. What we believe provides the assumptions of our thinking and of our acting, and therefore determines the quality of our relationships with God and with other persons.

iii. We must pray. Prayer is the inward attitude of faith and the continuing renewing of faith. Prayer means keeping oneself aware of God; prayer means keeping oneself aware of the essential individuality, personality, need and potential of other persons. Prayer enables us to receive from others and give to others in that glorious reciprocity that is the love-flow between the Father and the Son; the love-flow we call Holy Spirit.

Jesus in St John's Gospel prays for us like this:

Holy Father, keep them in thy name which thou hast given me: that they may be one even as we are one. . . . Sanctify them in the truth; thy word is truth. . . . For their sakes I sanctify myself, that they themselves also may be sanctified in truth.

For their sakes I sanctify myself. (John 17: 11-19).

Make that your motto and your motive on your journey and you will become a true inward Christian. Do this and your prayer will grow. Your prayer will cease to be centred on yourself and will become centred on God and on other people. Our prayer for others will become very simple. It will grow out of the perception that just as I am near to God, so is God near to these other persons who are my companions of the way - both those I like and those I dislike; and those who dislike me and those who unaccountably like me. We shall therefore always come to any other and receive any other who comes to us within this 'spiritual place' which is God's nearness to them and God's nearness to us. As they are under the eyes of his love, so they must be under the eyes of our love. For our very capacity to love is our awareness that we ourselves are loved by God.

The prayer we call intercession, prayer for others, belongs here. Our love for the person we are praying for is united with God's love for that same person. We are not concerned to produce an effect. We are allowing ourselves to become more aware of what is already the fact - namely that God is immediately and intimately present both to ourselves and to the ones for who we are praying. Our task is to hold the awareness of this fact in the still centre of our being.

Keep us O Lord in the joy, the simplicity, and the compassionate love of the gospel: bless us now and those whom you have given into our care; through Jesus Christ, our Lord.

Life Alone and Life Together

I

This cluster of buildings at Pilsdon in these Dorset valleys and hills has been a refuge over the years for all kinds of people. They have come as individuals in search of themselves, in search of others, in search of healing, in search of hope, in search of love, in search of life together - and whether or not they have been able to give a name to the object of their search, they have come in search of the meaning of the mystery of themselves - the baffle and the pain - the desire and the longing.

I do not know anything about you as individuals, but perhaps in what I have just said you recognise something of what first brought you here - some of you many years ago - in search of a refuge, of a home, of a new start. Pilsdon is a place of search, a place of exploration; and because individuals find themselves here in company with other individuals, Pilsdon is, above all, a place of experiment in living together.

But if the daily news and the evidence of past history teach us anything, they teach us that living together is the thing that human beings find most difficult to do. Conflicts and wars have always marked the history of the human race. Growth in population, the need for more land for cattle and crops to feed a growing population, envy of the better territory occupied by neighbouring tribes, such basic human needs and urges lead to aggression and conflict. Always there have been refugees - men, women and children fleeing along roads and tracks with a few possessions: and during this twentieth century, which we are pleased to call civilised, we have heard about and lived through the most terrible wars; and there is hardly a nation anywhere in the world which has not received refugees from elsewhere.

II

But conflict nearer home is also part of our experience: conflict between husband and wife, between parent and child, between worker and employer, between members of different races. Violence and terrorism are, it seems, an inescapable ingredient in our experience.

But conflict does not always express itself in physical violence: often in the more intimate circles of home and family and neighbourhood, or in a work or leisure group, conflict expresses itself in more interior ways - changing moods, sullen silence, rejecting looks, feelings of resentment, feelings of jealousy, feelings of bitterness, feelings of hatred. And often these hurt feelings, these rejecting feelings arise uninvited within us and we feel powerless to resist them or to get rid of them.

So complex are we as human beings that living together in peace, co-operation, happiness, is not always something that comes naturally or easily. Learning to live together is always something of an experiment: Pilsdon is a place where this experiment in living together is its reason for existing.

I suppose that at the root of our difficulties as human beings is the fact that we each tend to judge what happens by the way it affects ourselves rather than by the way it affects other people. We are self-centred rather than other-centred, and living together requires that we become more other-centred and less self-centred: concerned for the true well-being of others, not always waiting for others to be concerned for what we regard as our own well-being. We get into this state of mind at the start when we are babies and the object of admiration. We judge what happens by the pleasure or the pain we experience. Unless we can get free from this infantile reaction to what happens we shall not only be unhappy ourselves but cause unhappiness to others. That was easy enough for me to say: but I have no illusions about the difficulties that many of us have in achieving this inner revolution of attitude.

III

Community - people living together in peace and mutual goodwill - requires that each individual shall have his or her primary attention and loyalty focused beyond his or her own self-interest. We can only see ourselves as we really are and see other people as they really are if we have learned to see ourselves from a viewpoint outside of ourselves. Blessed are those who have no illusions about themselves for then they will be better able to see other people as they really are.

I want to say that I believe the teaching of Jesus, the stories he told and his whole personal approach to people and his own life of obedience to what he saw to be his Father's will - I believe the intention of Jesus in all he did and said was to help people to get rid of their illusions: to see things as they really are and not to impose their own limited interpretations on the situation. In all the Gospels there is emphasis on healing the blind so that they can see the world as it is. And when Jesus spoke of blindness he did not only mean physical blindness - the loss of visual eyesight - he meant an inner blindness, an inability to see people in a true light. His desire was to set people free from false views of themselves - and false distorted views of other people.

Over the years as I've listened to all sorts of people talking to me about their difficulties, I've been made aware of a widespread tendency in people to reject themselves, to blame themselves, to hate themselves; and if people cannot accept themselves and believe in themselves they are likely to be on the defensive, afraid to be open with other people. Aggressive behaviour, surly language is often the reaction of a person who is afraid or badly hurt. I remember a conversation with a woman in early middle life who came regularly to talk with me about her difficulties in coping with her work: she was a medical scientist. She had had a painful upbringing: her father used to beat her. She got herself to university and took a good degree and was working happily in hospital, fell in love with a young barrister, was engaged and then he jilted her. This emotional rejection aroused the hidden unhealed hurts of her father's treatment of her and she came to a full stop. She could not carry on. Gradually as we talked, she gained the confidence to finish a doctoral thesis and eventually achieved a responsible appointment in a hospital. Then one day she came to see me and all her self-rejecting seemed to have surged up again. At the end of this difficult conversation I said to her that I wanted her to do something. 'Write on a post card "I'm all right" and stick it on your mirror and every morning when you are doing your hair look straight into your eyes in the mirror and say what's on the card: "I'm all right".'

'I can't do that', she said in some alarm. 'I can never look at myself'. 'But you use a mirror for doing your hair?' 'Yes, but I never look myself full in the eyes'. 'Do that', I begged her. And so gradually she was able to overcome her rejection of herself based on her pain of being rejected by father and fiancé: she was able to accept herself and believe in herself. And so she became able to make better relations with other people.

I tell you this because I believe this inability to accept oneself is one of the causes of difficulty in making good relationships with others - creating difficulty in living together.

The more free we become in ourselves from illusions and fears and the emotional hangovers of earlier years, the more free we are to see other people as they really are. And that makes reconciliation more possible: it makes forgiveness more possible.

All this setting free I believe needs the context of a Christian community, where each person is accepted and listened to and cared for, until they become able to accept themselves in the liberating knowledge that they are accepted. What Jesus Christ brings into any and every group of people is the reassurance of the love of God. Once we can acknowledge that we are loved and accepted by God we are able to see ourselves and other people in a new light. We no longer withdraw into ourselves in fear: we are able to reach out to others in love. No longer the clenched fist with which to defend, but the open hand with which to welcome and embrace.

May Pilsdon, may the Christ who is present at Pilsdon continue to unclench our fists and open our hands, as we stretch them out in every Eucharist to receive the bread of life and the wine of love, as we reach out with hands of compassion to soothe another's pain.

Springs of Hope I

I

Hope is an elusive lady. When you try to describe her, to define her, she plays hard to get.

I cannot expect to succeed in this pursuit of hope on which I am venturing - but perhaps the value lies in the pursuit if it leads to some better understanding of this second of the three heavenly graces - Faith, Hope and Charity. To call hope, as some do, the Cinderella of the three heavenly graces may indicate that she is the most neglected in Christian discourse - but to call hope the Cinderella is hardly complimentary to faith and charity who bear no resemblance to the Ugly Sisters of the story.

But if hope is neglected in Christian discourse it is because she is so elusive, so hard to get, so mercurial to the touch. The cynic, I suppose, would tell us that we are pursuing a will o'the wisp, an illusion of the human heart, if we set off on this quest. Hope, the cynic would say, has no reality: she is the child of that self-deception that we humans are so good at - we whistle in the dark to keep up our courage, ourselves creating the sound which gives us a sense of companionship, a feeling of not being alone in the dark.

But the Lady Hope has a secure place in literature as well as in life whatever the cynic may say. Two columns in the index of the *Oxford Book of Quotations*: even more examples in Young's *Concordance of the Bible*. Perhaps we may say for a start that hope has something to do with desire and something to do with expectation. Desire and expectation are certainly ingredients: but I want to suggest something more profound, more fundamental, something deeply embedded in the very nature of things.

The regular rhythms of the energies of the universe, of this planet, of this order of nature are so reliable, so dependable that we feel confident in expecting that the sun will rise tomorrow as it has done in every twenty-four hours of our living experience. Day follows night: the longest of sleepless nights yields eventually to dawn. Spring, summer, autumn, winter follow one from another totally independently of ourselves. The alternations of the order of nature create an undergirding of confidence. It is no wonder that an eclipse of the sun would cause dismay to our primitive ancestors. Galileo's telescope produced panic not so long ago. But even violent disturbances such as earthquake or tornado do not wholly destroy this confidence. We know that these are exceptional interruptions and that the good order can be expected to continue beneath and beyond the interruptions. I want to suggest that the dependability of the ordered sequences of the rhythms of nature are one of the springs of hope. Predictable regularity of the energies and rhythms of the universe creates in human beings a basically hopeful expectation towards the future.

Hope is an ingredient in the givenness of life, like a figured base in an oratorio.

II

If we were to reflect more on the predictable, dependable elements in the givenness of life, in the rhythms of nature, we would be less vulnerable to the interruptions.

Similarly a knowledge of world history: world history is largely made up of unpredictable intrusions into the more ordered policies and patterns of states and nations; world history on a long view is seen as a continuing recovery after disaster, rebuilding after ruination, renaissance after disintegration. Decline of Greece, rise of Rome: decline of Rome, rise of Medieval: decline of Medieval, rise of Renaissance and Modern. If every experiment in human civilisation has within it the seeds of its own eventual decay, so too does it have within it the seeds of fresh beginnings: the phoenix rises from the ashes of the phoenix. What archaeologists do is to dig trenches through the mounds made of deposits of the past and identify in the sides of the trenches the layers which can be clearly seen to show a new effort rising on the failure of the old.

All this that I am saying is summed up in the inscription carved on the tomb of a Royalist knight who in the dark days of the Commonwealth built a new church in Leicestershire. The inscription reads:

> Whose singular praise it was to
> > have done the best things in the worst times
> And to have hoped them
> > in the most calamitous.

It would seem that in the order of nature and in the order of human nature there is a movement forwards that is fundamentally reliable: recovery after failure; renewal after destruction. On the basis of this confidence we make our daily choices, decisions, plans. Hope, it seems, is an attitude springing from the very nature of things, something much more lasting and dependable than our personal choice: quite other than mere wishful thinking. Along with energies making for destruction there are also counteravailing energies making for restoration and renewal.

So I would want to anchor the reality of hope in the fact of Creation. We live in a world where there is immeasurable pain and suffering: cruelty, fear, injustice, blind unreason, folly, greed, brutal tyranny and senseless destruction. But also there is much that is good, enabling, life-enhancing. There is the everlasting beauty of earth, sea and sky. From my study window I look out upon sunsets of indescribable loveliness - the Cathedral, the cedar tree and the Close houses silhouetted against a flaming background. There is also the man-made beauty of art, architecture, music, literature: there is love, generosity, courage: kindliness and laughter, wisdom and learning - and all these existing in the same world as the pains and horrors. The oppositions never cancel each other out. But there always seems enough of blessing and virtue even in the worst of times to enable our own continuance and renewal. Above all there is the miracle of life itself - of vitality and joy - surely a God-given gift. For life clearly comes from outside ourselves and cannot be accounted for by human reasoning.

In the dark days of Stalin's Russia there were candles to

freedom kept alight by such men as Pasternak and Solzhenitsyn and millions of unknown others, prisoners of conscience against all reason. In the dark days of Hitler's Ger-
many there were men like Pastor Niemoeller and Dietrich
Bonhoeffer and millions of unknown others who died in
Hitler's prisons and gas-chambers. We have all read deeply
moving accounts of ordinary men and women who did the best
things in the worst times and hoped them in the most calami-
tous.

III

But let us stay for a little longer with the world of nature - the
world of the peasant and the countryman, on whose bent backs
every civilisation has been built - a world from which too
many human beings in our times have become separated by
the distance between the world of nature and the huge con-
glomerations in which the majority of people now live.

Perhaps the most sinister words that have been uttered in
this century are those of the famous ocean explorer Jacques
Cousteau: 'The oceans are dying'. Rachel Carson's book
Silent Spring written over twenty years ago began to uncover
the facts about the effects of industry on man's natural environment. Another great prophet of this century, Albert
Schweitzer uttered terrible words, 'Man has lost his capacity
to foresee and forestall. He will end by destroying the earth'.
The possibility of nuclear holocaust has been added to the
poisoning of the environment. Acid rain is destroying forests
and buildings alike.

Those men who wrote the books of the Old Testament
lived close to nature: they knew that they had to dance in time
with the rhythms of the natural world; that nature had to be
respected and conserved. For them the natural world was the
theatre of God's glory. Every morning during Lent at matins
we say the Benedicite - that marvellous hymn of praise in
which nature is understood in all its variations as a praise of the
Creator.

Gradually that sense of the unity of man and nature has
been lost. From the seventeenth century onwards the world

came to be thought of as a vast and elaborate machine. The protests of such visionaries as William Blake were ridiculed. Man was now priding himself as being the master of things. Nature was seen as something exterior to himself and his own nature: it became a thing to be used and exploited. Scientists explored the mechanics and gained increasing control of the stored-up energies. The man in the white coat - laboratory man - became the priest of the new world. Technology would in time overcome all man's ills.

But that optimism is over: the unintended effects of scientific exploitation of nature have raised doubts in our minds and fear in our hearts. Advances in technology produce fear as well as benefit. We have begun to see that the benefits of science-based technology have been achieved at the expense of much of the world of nature on which human survival in the end will always depend. Motives of power or greed have overridden respect for, and care of, the fundamental earth realities.

So in this amazing way in which human beings have so often as individuals or as nations needed to be brought to the brink of disaster before they will see the truth of what they are doing, there is now all over the world an increasingly informed criticism and protest and a demand for a totally new understanding of what makes for our true well-being. There are voices like that of the Lutheran theologian Jurgen Moltmann who has written:

Man is not just the creature made in the image of God, standing over against the non-human creation of God as its master: rather he stands together with all other living things in the ongoing process of a creation which is still open and incomplete.

Slowly, strugglingly a new philosophy is beginning to enter the minds of thinking people - a new way of thinking about the truth of the way things are: a way of thinking which is becoming securely based in a scientific analysis, a way of thinking about the nature of things called ecology. It proclaims the interrelatedness of all nature and all human nature:

interrelatedness, interdependence and not separation, not endless specialisation. Someone said of the specialist that he is one who knows more and more about less and less.

At the natural level I find this new way of thinking, which is really the recovery of an ancient way of thinking that the modern world has lost - I find this new emphasis on integration and respect for the relatedness of man and nature, of animals and plants - I find this new ecological thinking one of the most refreshing springs of hope in a world that has almost brought itself to disaster by its refusal to recognise a fundamental truth about the way things really are.

Much progress has been made in diminishing the damage of the chemical effluence of industry and of mechanised farming by the efforts of conservationists. Inevitably there is here a conflict of interests, but at best conservation is ambulance work not full restoration of health. Health can only come as a result of everybody getting their thinking right about the interrelation of man and nature. This right thinking is already coming from an unblinkered view of reality among scientists. But even in this secular world I dare to say that only a recovery of a belief in creation, of the God-given relationship, can really restore the world's health. Christians should be in the forefront of this recovery of a whole and wholesome view of man's place in the world and open up again this clogged-up spring of hope.

Springs of Hope II

I

I began this exploration by proposing that hope is part of the givenness of life itself. Far from being what a cynic might call 'wishful thinking' or 'whistling in the dark to keep up your courage', hope, as I see it, is an ingredient in life and as such deeply rooted.

We considered the regularity and reliability of the rhythms of nature - night and day, seedtime and harvest - the four seasons changing without any contribution from ourselves: all this regularity providing a basic confidence on the strength of which we can make choices and decisions. We considered the rise and fall of successive experiments in civilisation during the centuries of mankind's long march. Dark days are not for ever: even a Stalin, even a Hitler eventually dies. The rising energies of new generations lead on to change, sometimes violent, sometimes gradual, by reformation or by revolution the 'old order changeth giving place to new'. All this long experience of nature and of history provides support for that basic attitude of hopefulness towards the future which corresponds with the vitality of ever-rising generations of men and women.

The latest period of western civilisation - in which you and I have been set to live our lives - began in the seventeenth century. Western man began to explore his own environment with new interest. New questions were asked about the universe and the place within it of planet Earth. The invention of the telescope and of the microscope opened up roads into new knowledge. The old Biblical view of the way things came to be what they are was gradually discarded in favour of the new story of human origins being told in ever-increasing detail by scientists. From being more or less at the mercy of energies he could not control, western man became more and more skilled at changing his environment to suit himself. One invention followed another and confidence grew in the prospect of a future in which science-based technology would solve all problems and bring the utopia. Hope built itself up on human reason and human skill.

The first major shock to this optimism was the First World War with its ghastly carnage of young lives - civilised western man destroying civilised western man. Aldous Huxley was one of the writers who began to challenge the optimism based on man's own abilities to solve all problems. The *Brave New World* as he saw it was far from the desirable paradise of popular expectation. The Second World War served only to increase the cynicism and disenchantment. Hiroshima was a turning point for the worse. The great achievements of scientists and technologists which seemed to hold out the promise of an enhanced quality of life were at the same time threatening that life with hideous destruction and imposing moral burdens that weighed down the spirit. A spreading sense of meaninglessness began to take the place of utopian optimism. A literature of despair, sometimes cynical, sometimes angry, grew up with its variation - a literature of the absurd. Camus, Brecht, Beckett are names we all know; we've all read Orwell's *Nineteen Eighty Four*. Camus spoke of 'our miserable and magnificent existence', highlighting the paradox and contradiction between achievement and threats of disaster. As long ago as 1938, Camus wrote:

> There is but one truly serious philosophical problem and that is suicide. Judging whether life is or is not worth living amounts to answering the fundamental question of philosophy.

André Malraux summed up the predicament of our humanity: 'In a world without God, life becomes absurd: death makes the point'. T.S. Eliot drew a similar conclusion - without God 'Hope will be hope for the wrong thing'. Can we who believe in God discover how to speak into the hopelessness and emptiness and despair of our contemporaries? This is what Paul saw as the gift of Christ - his power to rescue those who have 'no hope, being without God in the world'.

II

Earlier I was urging the need for us to recover a stronger sense of our relationship with the earth and all living plants and animals. And when I spoke of the confidence that is communicated to us from the orderliness and regularity and reliability of the energies and rhythms of nature, I was in fact speaking about the patterning of our world and our universe by our Creator. I believe we should acknowledge the regularity and dependability of the order of nature as evidence of the presence of the Creator within his continuing creation. I believe, too, that we should acknowledge the presence of the Creator in the ever-fresh energising of human history with every new generation of human beings. I do not think of God as a manipulator of the world from outside it: I think of God as working within the world he has made and himself limited by the structures of the order of nature. Those agonising questions people ask when faced with natural disasters: Why does God allow this? Why doesn't God prevent this? Can there be any God if this can happen? Those agonising questions imply an idea of God as an arch-manipulator capable of interfering with the outworkings of natural energies. But such a God would be capricious, creating uncertainty not confidence, bewilderment not hope. God working within and through the *necessary regularities of nature* is a God in whom I can believe; a God made powerless by his very gift of freedom to man and autonomy to nature: powerless in the sense of not interfering with the regularities of the world: but powerful in his working with, within and through those regularities.

In the eighth chapter of his letter to the Romans, Paul seems to me to be grasping for this kind of understanding. God by his presence within the ordered patterning of nature provides human beings with a foundation of confidence, a predisposition of hope. (Romans 8:18-28, 37-39).

III

Modern physics, chemistry and biology leave us in no doubt that we humans are of the earth earthy. We are made of the same stuff as the universe. But when the physicist, the chemist, the biologist, the sociologist and psychologist have said everything they can say descriptively about us, they have not said all there is to be said. What makes each of us unique is being a self-conscious, self-aware centre of experiences, feelings, hurts, decisions that are uniquely our own. Nobody can know my innermost self, unless I choose to disclose my innermost self to another. And as we all know, nothing is more difficult to do than to express in words our deepest feelings even when we want to. No matter how truly one person may love another person, neither can ever become the centre of the self-awareness of the feeling self of the other.

So to this self-aware personal centre of interior and exterior experiences, to this everyman who cannot live by himself or herself alone, but must relate to others and communicate with others in order to survive: to this personal centre which is the 'I' of each of us - God speaks. That remarkable collection of writings we have inherited from the Hebrews - the writings of the Old Testament - is all about the Creator addressing created persons, using the means of communication summed up in the expression, *the Word*. The Hebrews knew themselves to be addressed by a mysterious other from beyond themselves. Sometimes they related this experience in the form of stories, sometimes by the more direct method of speech: the writings of the prophets are impossible to place in any other literary category than their own. 'Thus saith the Lord'. How the prophets heard the word they spoke we are not told. But they spoke with deep authority - in judgment, in encouragement, in hope. There was an incarnation of the Divine Word in the prophets before the unique incarnation of the Divine Word in Jesus when that Word which was God's Word became flesh and lived on earth in a particular place, at a particular time, to a particular group of people. Some hung upon his words: others plotted to get rid of the man who spoke those words, and hung him on a cross.

Shall we not be right to say that creation and incarnation are two parts of a single action of God? He makes us out of the chemical components of the planet Earth, and as we develop our self-awareness he speaks to us through the insights of others to whom he has spoken - others who have listened and have heard. And then at the culminating moment he speaks to us in his living Word, in a form and a language we can all understand and to which we can all respond - in human form and in human language - in this man Jesus of Nazareth who was crucified.

This Word of God incarnate, this Jesus, is above all else to us a word of hope. He lifts our eyes towards a new vision of what we have it in us to become. He teaches us of what spirit we are: he reveals to us our destiny as children of God. But this supernatural destiny does not stand as a contradiction of our natural existence: he speaks of our destiny as of our being drawn to our fulfilment in and through our natural existence as the only conclusion of that existence. Everything that happens to us is grist to the mill of our growth in holiness, wholeness. All the hurts, failures, frustrations, as well as the joys, achievements, loves, are to be gathered into that wholeness, that 'glorious liberty of the children of God'. The godlikeness which is the fulfilment of our nature is not something that can be seized or stolen as in the ancient legend of Prometheus; nor something that can be bought in the modern legend of Faust. All is of grace - God's working in us with our willing co-operation. Our hope in the deepest sense lies in our response to that action of God which is called creation and incarnation; and more particularly our hope is in that person, Jesus, who was crucified and yet continues with us as an animating presence enabling our growth. Which brings us to that spring of hope expressed in the passage of Paul's letter to the Colossians:

'The secret is this: Christ in you, the hope of a glory to come.'

And he adds:

'To this end I am toiling strenuously with all the energy and power of Christ at work in me.' (1: 27-29).

Springs of Hope III

I

So far in our search for springs of hope we have traced sources in several places - in the regularity and dependability of the patterning of the primal energies of nature; in the ever-recurring birth of children and the will of parents to have children even in dark times; in the continuing re-birth of civilisations; in our spiritual growth as human persons from the basic chemical conglomerate of our biological structure; in our capacity for self-transcendence; in our self-awareness; in our ability to distinguish between good and evil and to discern what is true from what is false. If we weren't so accustomed to ourselves we would be continually amazed that so much could develop from such unlikely embryonic beginnings. What a thing is man, indeed!

We have also noted how necessary for all this human development have been the regularities and dependability of the world structures of the order of nature. Without the confidence that, except in seismic places, the ground under our feet is solid and that day will follow night, we would never be able to make choices or decisions or plans.

I find it impossible to believe that all this is an accident - the chance result of some prehistoric 'big bang' - or what someone called 'the fortuitous concatenation of atoms'. The story told by modern scientists of the origins of the universe and the emergence of biological organisms, for all its fascination, only takes us so far into an understanding of the way things are. The science-story does not account for the mystery element in human experience. The answer to the question *How*? does not touch the question *Why*? and *For what*?

So in spite of its difficulties, I have to use theological language, language of creation and incarnation, language of God. Otherwise we are left with the absurdity of which Camus and Sartre and Beckett and others were writing in the mid-decades of this century. But if we are to use theological language as a clue to the interpretation of the mystery and meaning of being alive and being human we have to seek a way of using theological language that acknowledges the reality of the story the scientists now tell us. Theologians like Don Cupitt and David Jenkins, and at an earlier date John Robinson, are struggling to be honest to God and honest about God in the world as we now know it to be.

II

As I have indicated earlier, I cannot use language of God as creator which is incompatible with the language of God as incarnate which has developed out of the Christ-event and centuries of Christian reflection on the meaning of the Christ-event. God incarnate in Christ Jesus is God placing himself wholly within the play of circumstance, making himself obedient within the things he suffered and thereby giving evidence of his indestructible reality. For what God incarnate in Jesus Christ demonstrates in the actual circumstances of a human historical life is the reality of a kind of love which evil cannot destroy, because all that evil can do to this kind of love is to give this love ever fresh opportunities of loving. 'When he was reviled he did not revile in return'. The powerlessness of God is the evidence of his power - the power not of a potentate but of a lover who loves to the uttermost. As incarnate he addresses us with his Word to elicit our response - his Word spoken through prophets as a preparation for his Word made flesh in the person of Jesus. He gives autonomy to the order of nature which is the subject matter that scientists study. He beckons into freedom the human beings who uniquely exist by the same natural energies in the form of self-aware creatures capable both of good and of evil. As the author of the letter to the Hebrews expressed it:

> In many and various ways God spoke of old to our fathers
> by the prophets; but in these last days he has spoken to us
> by a Son, whom he appointed the heir of all things,
> through whom also he created the world. He reflects the

glory of God and bears the very stamp of his nature, upholding the universe by his word of power. (1: 1-4).

I take this to mean that God relates to us both in the reliability of the order of nature and in the confrontation of our consciousness with his Word in order to give us freedom and to call us into an exercise of freedom that is creative of true relationships in society with other people. The concept of his Kingdom is a concept of relationships, of the ideal city.

III

This is, I believe, the Christian understanding of the meaning and purpose of this risky business of life as we know it. And here lies the strongest case against God. The strongest case against God is not the case of credibility: it is the case of immorality. The moral issue is the real challenge to credibility. Will the end be seen to justify the means? Can all this human pain, suffering, frustration, isolation, poverty, hunger, cruelty that makes up the world's giant agony, can all this when put into the final scales of reckoning be seen to have been justified by the end result? This for me is and always has been - for me as for many others - the real testing point of faith. Paul voiced such a faith when he wrote:

I consider that the sufferings of this present time are not worth comparing with the glory that is to be revealed to us. (Rom. 8: 18).

But what glory could there be that would make it possible to say at the end of time: 'Yes it was all worthwhile.' Can any final glory redeem Auschwitz? What springs of hope are there for us when we honestly face the horror of the pain involved in this whole human experiment?

Having made out the case for the sufficient reliability of the order of nature to make possible the development of human freedoms, I have to go on to say that, nevertheless, life deals the cards capriciously. Some people are given a flying start and others a crippling handicap. Some people grow into wonderful, sensitive and loving characters and others become capable of exquisite and monstrous cruelty. No one has exposed the human capacity for evil with deeper penetration than our near neighbour, William Golding. It is hardly surprising that this century has produced such atheistic exponents of despairing defiance as Camus, Russell, Sartre and the rest.

IV

Throughout Christian history this awful facet of human wickedness and the unfairness of circumstance and the consequent suffering of men and women has been met by a theology of hope of a life beyond death when the imbalance and injustices and anguish of experience in time will be transfigured from glory to glory.

What seems to have sustained the people of the Old Testament was not a hope of individual immortality but rather a hope of the continuation of the nation. Always there would be a remnant who would be saved through the fires of calamity. In Prophets and Psalms there are many expressions of a hope of God's rescue of his people. Here is that hope as expressed by the prophet Hosea:

That is why I am going to lure her and lead her out into the wilderness and speak to her heart.

I am going to give her back her vineyards and make the Valley of Misery a gateway of hope. (2: 14-15).

Only as the Hebrews developed a sense of the individual rather than primarily a sense of the tribe or nation do we find the beginnings of a hope of individual survival.

Through the centuries of the Christian Church there has been a strong hope of the fulfilment of God's purpose for the individual and the community on the other side of death. This hope has often been expressed in images and metaphors we find strange. Belief in an afterlife doesn't come easily to people today: indeed I wonder if ever before in human history have there been so many people who have decided that this life is all. Death is the end of the story.

Over against that is the deep Christian concern to justify the ways of God to man. And there is no way of pretending that the question I raised about the unfairness and injustice that are consequences of the kind of world we live in and the kind of people we are, is not a real and poignant question: a real question about the existence of God and about the goodness of God. Can God of all the earth be right if these sufferings are the inevitable and unresolvable consequences of his creative acts? I do not see that it is possible to believe in the God and Father of Our Lord Jesus Christ and deny any reality beyond death. If God is to carry out his allegedly loving purposes for all mankind then he needs more 'elbow room' than this lifetime alone can offer.

But mere survival of death holds no attraction. In which of my moods might I survive? Life beyond death only holds attraction if it means a continuing spiritual growth and trans-formation until all selfishness and evil are changed into more love. This is the kind of expectation we find in the New Testament. This is the kind of future that inspired J.H. New-man's poem *The Dream of Gerontius*. What corrupts the thought of life beyond death is the thought of it in terms of reward or mere consolation for oneself - an attitude that aroused the suspicions of Simone Weil and the contempt of such an avowed atheist as Marghanita Laski. More to be commended is the attitude expressed in the seventeenth-century hymn:

My God, I love thee, not because
I hope for heaven thereby . . . .
Nor from the hope of gaining ought,
Nor seeking a reward:
But as thyself hast loved me
O ever-loving Lord.
So would I love thee, dearest Lord
And in thy praise will sing,
Solely because thou art my God
And my most loving King.

For myself I find it difficult to believe in life after death, but even more difficult not to. The absence of such a belief reduces the whole of human life ultimately to an absurdity. And the whole Gospel of Christ's resurrection would seem to demand it as the transfiguration and completion of all that has been endured and achieved during the years before; otherwise human existence would be an unfinished symphony or like a battlefield strewn with corpses. It would be difficult to affirm life, to pursue the spiritual path, if all meaning has to be contained within the confines of this present life and death is total extinction.

I remember vividly the words of a great theologian of my youth - Oliver Quick. After a lecture in which he wrestled with these problems he said:

Perhaps the most deeply Christian hope of our souls is that in heaven we may be able to say of all the evil in the world what we have already begun to say about the crimes of those who were responsible for Our Lord's death, namely, that, evil as they are, we could not now will them to have been otherwise, since even they have been made to bear their part in the triumph of God.

On this issue of ultimate hope let me say just this. I believe we must hope that such progress as we make in our lifetime towards God, towards holiness, will be carried through to fulfilment in a perfected relationship with God and with all others. But this distant hope should be a kind of descant to our life here and now. Here and now we are called to live by faith and to grow by grace into our own personal and individual Christlikeness so that God may reach out and touch the lives of others through us. The hope that we shall set before ourselves is the hope of being and becoming agents of the Divine Love in the world of our time.

Dust to Gold

I

Rise heart: thy Lord is risen. Sing his praise
Without delayes.
Who takes thee by the hand, that thou likewise
With him may'st rise:
That, as his death calcined thee to dust,
His life may make thee gold, and much more just.

Dust to gold: the ambition of the alchemist. This was the
search that captivated certain scientists in the middle ages - the
greed for gold, the search for a chemistry that would transform
baser metals into the gold of their greed's desire. Gold means
power. The lust for power, the lust for gold as instrument of
power, this lust is personified in the world's literature in the
characters of Prometheus and of Faust - this passion for power
lies at the root of most of the ills of human history. Passion for
power is the breeding ground of fear and all the cruelties
perpetrated by men in power who are afraid of losing power.
Fear is the foul virus of man's inhumanity to man.

Jesus was crucified by men in power, who feared in him a
threat to their security. According to the Fourth Gospel, Caiaphas the High Priest determined on Jesus' death for fear that
Jesus, if left free, would provoke the Romans to come and
destroy both their holy place and their nation. It was Caiaphas
also who played on the fear of Pontius Pilate, the Roman
governor: 'If you let this man go, you are not Caesar's friend.'
(John 19: 12).

Analyse the horror news that bombards our homes every
day by contrivance of information technology: analyse all this
wretched tale of the inability of human beings to live together
peaceably and you will find greed, lust for power and fear as
the festering fruit
Of that forbidden tree, whose mortal taste

133

Brought death into the world, and all our woe
With loss of Eden.

II

But Easter also is about alchemy. George Herbert uses this pregnant analogy in his Easter poem which I was quoting when I began to speak to you. Dust into gold; death into life; crucifixion into resurrection.

This Easter alchemy is of a different sort - not man's mad seeking of power but God's wonderful gift: God's transformation of the chemical conglomerate of the biological organisms that we are into such persons as human persons are capable of becoming - radiant centres of intelligence and love that transforms the dust of which we are made into beings 'much more just'. What a wealth of meaning Herbert finds packed into that little phrase 'much more just'. Gerard Manley Hopkins takes up this same small word:

The just man justices;
Keeps grace: that keeps all his goings graces;
Acts in God's eye what in God's eye he is -
Christ. For Christ plays in ten thousand places,
Lovely in limbs, and lovely in eyes not his
To the Father through the features of men's faces.

III

But this Easter alchemy which transfigures the primal earth-stuff of which we are made is a costly process. The Three Hours on Good Friday took us through an experience of costly grace as expounded in Mark's strange, spare, severe presentation of the Passion story. Everybody must be salted by fire. Without fire, no alchemy. *But*, what other interpretation of the human paradox and predicament which is both ourselves and our society goes more convincingly to the root of the matter than this story that has Jesus at its centre?

He lived in the world of his time, exposed to the play of circumstances as we live exposed to the accidents and upheavals of our own time. But when those men and women who were his close contemporaries reflected on his way of living and dying, on the things he said and did and in the manner in which he accepted and absorbed the violence and the desolation inflicted on him, they found themselves speaking of this particular man and his particular story as a universal symbol, the focus and pivot of a fresh and transforming interpretation of all human reality. Within a very few years Paul writing to the Christians at Colossae was presenting Christ as a cosmic reality.

Whatever happened to bring about this illumination of their understanding of the significance of Jesus - this experience they spoke of as resurrection - it was a conviction about his continuing presence. And the central core of that conviction was the return of the one who had been crucified to those who had crucified him - a return not in anger, not in condemnation, not in revenge, not in rejection but in what they could only call forgiveness. In spite of their betrayals, deceits and desertions they found themselves embraced by the one they had fled from. Whatever else the Easter story is about it is certainly about forgiveness, about the transformation of relationships, about the cancellation of fear, about the establishment of trust.

Whatever the actual experience those first friends of Jesus were speaking about in those incomparable Easter stories, the evidence of the truth of what they were saying was in themselves - the change in their whole outlook - the growth of new communities rapidly spreading through the Mediterranean world - a new way of living human life, forever renewing itself, rediscovering itself afresh century after century to our own time and this company, gathered to 'Sing his praise without delays.'

Each of the Easter stories in the varied telling of the Four Gospels is an affirmation of a restored relationship in a changed mode. In each there is a communication of forgiveness. To select one - St John tells it - his story of the restoration of Simon Peter whose fear for himself had caused him to deny Jesus three times. (John 21: 15-17).

On this rock of Peter's restoration is Christ's commission given to the Church. The Church community is to live in every place within the world's life in the knowledge of forgiveness mediated to the crucifiers by the crucified. Love that is rooted in the experience of being forgiven by the one who has been injured is the only love strong enough to be commissioned to bring this new life to others. To Peter, penitent and forgiven, the commission is given: 'Feed my sheep'. Only a Church community rooted in penitence and forgiveness can be a Church community able to keep Christ's kind of loving in circulation in our tortured world, trapped in fantasies. This is what it means to be Easter people - therefore;

Rise heart: thy Lord is risen. Sing his praise
Without delayes.
Who takes thee by the hand, that thou likewise
With him may'st rise:
That, as his death calcined thee to dust,
His life may make thee gold, and much more just.

Optional God?

I

Having reached a date well into my seventy-second year I find myself more sure of fewer things than I was sure of when I was an undergraduate. I'm absolutely sure that 'I am' and that 'I am to die', in all probability before I reach a hundred! But I have to confess that I do not find myself impelled with the same urgency which led Richard Baxter in the seventeenth century to write:

I preached as never sure to preach again,

And as a dying man to dying men.

The fact that I do not feel impelled with the same urgency as Richard Baxter says something about me, something about him and something about the cultural difference between his century and ours. This doesn't mean that I have any less concern about the mystery and meaning of being alive and being human, or about the urgency of the perennial human questions: 'Who am I?', 'What may I hope?', 'What should I do?'; or about the Christian Gospel in relation to these fundamentals. It indicates rather a degree of perplexity and enquiry that accompanies the commitment of faith and its communication to others in our so different world.

The acids of modernity have eaten away at many of the certainties which Baxter felt confident in proclaiming. Your preacher today, unable in truth's name to take his stand on a platform of Biblical fundamentalism, will no doubt sound tentative and exploratory to some of his hearers; whereas others who choose to attend a University Sermon in a spirit of search and enquiry may be the more helped on their way by a sincere recognition of the difficulties of expressing Christian belief convincingly in the intellectual and moral climate of our times.

What has been eroded in the last three centuries is the frame of reference within which previous generations were able to understand what was happening around them. This frame of reference had been developed and modified from roots in classical Greece, in ancient Israel and in continuing Christianity. But our western world today is a world organised as if it made no difference whether there were a God or not. Few people are prepared to say, 'There is no reality corresponding to the word God,' unless they have adopted the tenets of Marxism-Leninism. But most people in Europe do as a matter of fact organise their lives as if it made no difference whether there is a God or not. Those who choose the way of belief are free to do so. 'God' is tolerated as one of the options open to private individuals in their private lives. As far as public truth goes the framework of reference is secular.

II

But if we are to understand this phenomenon of European secularism we need to recognise that it is a post-Christian secularism. As the Scotsman said: 'Yes! I'm an atheist, but I'd have you know that I'm a Presbyterian atheist.' This western compromise in which people don't deny God's reality but act on the assumption that there is no God, has for many years been able to hold the western world together because we have accepted a basic common stock of agreed values. What is falling apart now is this consensus about a basic common stock of agreed values. It was in the aftermath of the First World War that the poet W.B. Yeats wrote the poem which begins:

> Turning and turning in the widening gyre
> The falcon cannot hear the falconer;
> Things fall apart; the centre cannot hold;
> Mere anarchy is loosed upon the world,
> The blood-dimmed tide is loosed, and everywhere
> The ceremony of innocence is drowned:
> The best lack all conviction, while the worst
> Are full of passionate intensity.

Since that was written we have suffered a Second World

War and embedded within it the gas-chambers of Auschwitz and Bergen-Belsen. Writing at the outset of the Nazi movement the Russian Christian philosopher Nicholas Berdyaev announced the *End of Our Time* and declared, 'Man without God is no longer man.' Recently George Steiner offered a searching and disturbing analysis of the impulse behind the *Shoah*, the holocaust. He argues that the Jew has been loathed and feared in the civilisation of the West not only as the murderer of Jesus but even more as the inventor of God, and therefore of conscience. He writes:

> It is when they are exhausted or degenerating the organs and muscle tissue secrete contagions and maleficent substances into the human body. So it was that the original Pauline and Patristic theology of Jew-hatred, together with the more general and even deeper-lying resentment of monotheism and sacrificial morality, took on their terrible, festering virulence precisely as Christianity and a belief in God as such began receding from the spiritual habits and intellectual-political adherence of Western civilisation. There is a perfect logic in the anti-semitism of a Voltaire. There is a clear pattern in the fact that the Auschwitz-world erupts out of the subconscious collective obsessions of an increasingly agnostic, even anti- or post-Christian society.

If Steiner is right in the diagnosis he puts forward, then it is not only Christianity that is being marginalised as a consequence of rationalist scepticism and criticism from the Enlightenment; the scientific achievements that have grown out of the new attitudes of the eighteenth-century philosophers and mathematicians are equally at risk. Everyday there are indications that we are living not only in a post-Christian world but in a world becoming increasingly sub-human. The enlightenment liberated the western world from dogmatic, authoritarian shackles. But we are seeing now that the undoubted intellectual, artistic, material benefits we enjoy from the critical explorations of those writers and the brilliant achievements of science-based technology that followed are themselves precarious, increasingly threatened by the misdirection of some of these same energies. The challenge to the claims of secular humanism to be an alternative framework of reference within which we can interpret what is going on around us in a post-Christian world - the challenge lies in the unintended but destructive results and potential of what secularised men and women are so eagerly doing.

The exponential escalation of world population is not a freak of nature. It is rather the unintended result of applying scientific methods of death-control in the Third World without any compensating birth-control, and planned provision of educational and technical help in developing adequate resources of water supply and food production. Rapid population increase is made worse by political and administrative mismanagement plus the uncontrollable vagaries of weather conditions. All this has contributed to those terrible human sufferings that have been televised into our homes. To this grim story we must add the destructive effects on the natural environment of chemical effluences from industrial enterprises and other side-effects of commercial exploitation of natural resources. Greed regardless of consequences to others is only one of the evils that follows from living in the world as if it were ours to do what we like with - as if there were no ultimate values to which we owe allegiance.

Who makes and sells all those guns that seem so readily available to rival gangs in the anarchistic hell that was once Beirut? Did those scientists whose researches led to the release of stored-up nuclear energy ever imagine any of the possible consequences of the success of their endeavours - the devastation of Hiroshima, the wind-distributed radioactive fountain of deadliness erupting from Chernobyl, or even those ever-increasing, ever-embarrassing barrels of radioactive nuclear waste? Is our human existence with all that is lovely and good and true within it doomed to be destroyed by the inadvertent cleverness of secular man?

The barbarians of old battered away at the gates of the citadels of civilisation. The new barbarians live within the citadels, masquerading as the prophets and precursors of a glossier future, trivialising and mocking the inherited wisdom of past ages - those values that underpin a genuinely human society. Does *can* inevitably imply *must* or even *may*? What about surrogate motherhood, *in vitro* fertilisation, embryo research, frozen zygotes?

III

Post-Christian secularism is a puzzling phenomenon: it is far from clear how to define the Churches' relation and duty towards it. The main Churches of Europe are severely handicapped by their own confusions and ambiguities in trying to understand their own nature and the nature of secularism. Nor in England does it appear that there is yet among the laity and clergy a sufficiently serious awareness of the situation. We have hardly begun to assimilate the new understanding of the character and authority of our Biblical title-deeds in the light of the critical studies of scholars for a century and more. I fear that all too few of those who could and should will actually read *The Futures of Christianity* by David Edwards. This masterly comprehensive study explores the varied circumstances of the Churches in all parts of the world with an especially searching study of the situation in Europe. One fact that emerges sharply is the contrast between the Christian confidence in parts of the world where Christianity is a relatively new experience, and the state of mind of Christians in a secularised environment where large numbers of people think they have grown beyond all that.

For many centuries in Britain Christians have made the running and set the pace, creating schools, colleges, universities, building hospitals, churches, cathedrals, influencing legislation and setting standards for social and personal behaviour. A great deal of the creativity remains - not least in the arts - in music, poetry, painting. But the spirit that stimulated this output is now a gentle breeze rather than a rushing, mighty wind.

Little by little the relegation of God to the category of optional has inevitably led to adjustments of the place of the Church in the estimate of the nation. A marginalised Church is now allotted a minor function, expected to devote itself to something called 'religion'. This wispy, insubstantial thing called 'religion' has little affinity with robust Christianity understood as a way of dealing with life, an interpretation of the mystery and meaning of being alive and being human, concerned with relationships at all levels, guardian of the purity of those pivotal words on which human existence turns - truth, justice, freedom, personality, love, spirituality, holiness - each word a 'precious cup of meaning'.

The other day the Archbishop of Canterbury asked the Cardinal Archbishop of Westminster what disturbed him most about the way things are. Dom Basil replied: 'Growing disregard for truth.' Archbishop Desmond Tutu of South Africa recently said: 'I don't understand what Bible people are reading when they say that Christianity has nothing to do with politics.'

In the trials and tribulations of the Soviet Union, of Poland, of the Warsaw Pact, of South Africa, of Uganda, of South America and elsewhere, Christians have been forced to decide where they really do stand. The faith of many has been strengthened under the hammer blows of persecution, as has been the case at all periods from the disintegrating years of the Roman Empire until our own times. Christianity is an anvil that has worn out many hammers. Secularism is a more insidious enemy: it works more like a virus; emasculating and weakening the fibres of mind and heart. The enemy within the gates of the citadel is less obviously an enemy than the one who is battering at the gates from outside.

If our Christianity is to out-think and out-live this secular culture which seems set towards self-destruction, then Christian men and women really must open their eyes and read the signs of the times, open their minds to the real message and meaning of Christ's life and teaching, open their hearts to that *AGAPE* - love - which alone makes possible the *KOINONIA* - community, open their hands to human need. We have to learn the art of being a vibrant minority, we have to discover the twenty-first century equivalent of those monastic communities which in Europe's dark ages christianised and civilised the energies of the invaders who filled the power vacuum left empty by the decline and fall of the Roman Empire.

IV

If you ask me what it means to me to be trying to follow a Christian path in this post-Christian intellectual and moral atmosphere, I can only reply that faith for me means allegiance to a kind of vision and response to a kind of claim. To repudiate either the vision or the claim would be nothing less than a betrayal of the core of my being.

As a twentieth-century man trying to live as a Christian in a society that seems less and less able to understand what Christianity is all about, when I ask myself what in the end and stripped of all secondary considerations I really believe in, I find I must say that I believe in the presence and power of a Love which is indestructible because its character is such that the worst that evil can do to such Love is to provide such Love with ever fresh opportunities of loving. I believe in the presence and power of this kind of Love because this is what I receive from the story in four perceptions that has at its centre Jesus Christ crucified and risen. I've seen evidence of this kind of Love in the lives of certain individuals and groups - past and present. I've discovered the truth of it in my own life - not by having achieved this kind of loving but by having failed to achieve it and yet knowing it to be achievable and more to be desired than anything else. Of all possible ways of setting about living as a human being in this world this is the only way that is self-evidently true because it authenticates itself.

I believe that in speaking like this I am speaking in my way and falteringly but none the less genuinely of that dynamic Reality and Claim to which Christians have always been directing men and women's attention when they try to speak to them about *GOD*.